# Brit-myth

Focus on Contemporary Issues (FOCI) addresses the pressing problems, ideas and debates of the new millennium. Subjects are drawn from the arts, sciences and humanities, and are linked by the impact they have had or are having on contemporary culture. FOCI books are intended for an intelligent, alert audience with a general understanding of, and curiosity about, the intellectual debates shaping culture today. Instead of easing readers into a comfortable awareness of particular fields, these books are combative. They offer points of view, take sides and are written with passion.

SERIES EDITORS
Barrie Bullen and Peter Hamilton

In the same series

# Brit-myth

## Who do the British think they are?

CHRIS ROJEK

REAKTION BOOKS

*For Little Luke: much bigger than he used to be*

Published by Reaktion Books Ltd
33 Great Sutton Street
London EC1V ODX, UK

www.reaktionbooks.co.uk

First published 2007

Printed and bound in Great Britain
by Cromwell Press, Trowbridge, Wiltshire

*British Library Cataloguing in Publishing Data*
Rojek, Chris
    Brit-myth: who do the British think they are? – (Focus on contemporary issues)
    1. National Characteristics, British  2. Great Britain – Social life and customs – 21st
    century  3. Great Britain – Foreign public opinion
    I. Title
    306'.0941

ISBN-13: 978 1 86189 336 9

# Contents

'We' is the most treacherous of the English pronouns

*Anthony Burgess*

# CHAPTER ONE

# Britons: A Declining Breed?

The 23rd British Social Attitudes Survey, published by the National Centre for Social Research in 2007, included a juicy morsel that provoked a media feeding frenzy (Park 2007). Less than half of Britain's inhabitants (44 per cent) saw fit to describe themselves as 'British'.

This finding is part of a long-established downward trend. In 1997, 52 per cent of all Britons described themselves as 'British'. The apparent desertion of British nationalism by the British themselves runs counter to common, intuitive international stereotypes of the British as 'arrogant', 'superior' and 'excessively proud' of their culture and history. It begs the timely question: in the post-Empire/European Union context, who do the British think they are? This question is the central issue of this book.

The rate of decomposition in British identity appears to be most alarming in England. The cartoon caricature John Bull was created by John Arbuthnot in 1712, as the quintessence of the kingdom of Great Britain. However, a precedent was swiftly established in Scotland, Wales and Ireland to dismiss him as the personification of the English: all roast beef, bitter, bluff heartiness, hypocrisy and greed. Historical conditions tempered the expres-

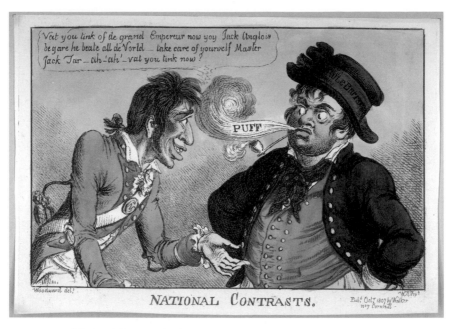

'National Contrasts', 1807

sion of this perspective. For example, at the height of Empire, and when Britain 'stood alone' during the Second World War, the Scottish, Welsh and Irish populations were prepared to suppress nationalist issues on pragmatic grounds. The British Empire provided unprecedented opportunities for upward mobility and the accumulation of wealth. After the First World War, the evident decline of Empire unbuttoned nationalist sympathies. This was expressed most cogently in the campaign for Irish home rule – the violence of this struggle overshadowed Scottish and Welsh initiatives for independence. For over 90 years the tea leaves on the question of British nationalism came up in one direction: towards the devolution and separatism that threaten the lifeblood of the Union. The findings of the 23rd British Social Attitude survey indicate that the English are finally catching up with their Scottish, Welsh and Irish cousins in choosing to discard 'British' as an acceptable term to express national solidarity. For John Bull and his ilk, who, after all, must be considered deathless British loyalists, the conclusion is miserable: the British are a declining breed.

The media presented two main reasons to explain the waning of British nationalism. Firstly, New Labour's devolution of civil, economic and political powers from Westminster to new national assemblies in Edinburgh, Cardiff and Belfast was credited with providing a spur to Scottish, Welsh and Northern Irish nationalism. The strengthening of nationalist identity in Scotland, Wales and Northern Ireland was achieved at the expense of weakening support for traditional ideas of Britain and Britishness. By the same token, devolution was posited as the reason for the resurgence of nationalism in England. Faced with substantial home rule in Edinburgh, Cardiff and Belfast, the English began to covet nationalist powers for themselves. Some regions, notably Cornwall, have gone further in articulating the case for independence. The house of cards upon which Britain has stood since the Act of Union in 1707 suddenly appears more fragile and rickety than ever.

Secondly, the idea of Britishness was now seen as tainted with negative associations with the British Empire. For many British citizens, conscious of living in a postcolonial world, it is now dreadfully uncool to adhere to the nationalist idea of Britishness. For over two centuries it was deployed to legitimize slavery, illegal invasion, the forced expropriation of wealth and the imprisonment of critics and foes. Many Britons now feel that these atrocities outweigh the claim of apologists – like the contemporary conservative historian, Niall Ferguson – that, on balance, the Empire ought to be regarded as a force for good. Evidently, in a spectacular denial of roots, many British citizens today are perfectly happy to consider themselves to be English, Scottish, Welsh or Northern Irish without wishing to carry any of the baggage of Empire.

Viewed over the last 250 years, this is a *volte-face* in national outlook. At the high-water mark of Empire, Britishness was regarded as the combination of 'the best and highest' that nature and nurture could provide in the British

Isles. It was as if each nation was believed to provide crucial elements that the others lacked. The marriage between Scottish invention and discipline, Irish daring and imagination, Welsh decency and pluck, and English application and genius for compromise may have been a shotgun foursome. However, it was blessed with providence. In the nineteenth century and right up to the 1920s and '30s, the British believed that British pan-nationalism was both an irresistible force and the envy of the world.

Yet the postwar period has turned this imperial logic upon its head. Critical post-imperial history, developed both from the Commonwealth and within Britain, presents Empire as an era of dubiously won fortune and shameful history. Its legacy is not providence and pride, but apology and regret. On this account, Empire was not Britain's glory, but a stain on her history.

The decline in British nationalism – and divided feelings about the British Empire – raise the issue of what 'being British' means today. One of the greatest challenges facing a modern British government is the task of reconciling nationalism with multiculturalism, multi-ethnicity and globalization. This goes well beyond engineering compliance between migrant populations and hallowed British traditions. Many native-born Britons feel distanced from the content and style of the customary narrative of national belonging. The findings of the 2007 Ajegbo Report on nationalism, multi-ethnicity and education make for salutary reading on this matter. The Commission set out to assess how schooling might assist children from multi-ethnic backgrounds to forge strong links with the ideal of Britishness. However, as the inquiry progressed it became apparent that the problem of conflicted national identity was not restricted to migrant, ethnic populations. Many ethnic British are equally confused about who they are and where they stand – in areas of mixed ethnic composition their children often suffer labelling and discrimination that leaves them feeling themselves to be strangers in their own land.

Educationalists and politicians have responded in a predictable but unsatisfactory fashion. Free speech, tolerance, responsibility and respect for the law are bruited as definitive, cohesive British values, won by the struggles of ordinary British people and preserved zealously as the birthright of every Briton, irrespective of race, religion, creed or colour. Put a dozen British people in the same room, it is claimed, and they will forget their differences as they hail their momentous heritage of Runnymede, Tolpuddle and Dunkirk.

There are two things wrong with the strategy of using 'traditional' British values to overcome the frictions and tensions associated with multi-culturalism, multi-ethnicity and pan-Europeanism today. Firstly, traditional British values are slippery abstractions. Many people find it hard to identify with the ideals of free speech, responsibility and tolerance. Often it is only when these ideals are infringed or violated that they become a cause célèbre; most of the time they are not experienced as the historical achievement of resistance and struggle but rather as the unremarkable, 'given' grain of every-day life. Secondly, one measure of the global influence of Empire is that these values are no longer recognized as distinctively 'British'. In their modern form, they may have been overhauled from Greek and Roman precedents, then transformed by British struggles and the 'genius' for British compromise. But today they are universally adopted in all Western nation-states, as 'sacred' in the United States, Australia, New Zealand, Canada, the European Union, South Africa and India as in the British Isles.

Ethnic migration and multiculturalism have transformed the face and character of Britain. Some Britons have difficulty in acknowledging the change; together with many Anglophiles abroad, they resort to a romantic 'Merrie England' view, which is extended to cover the entire nation. On this account, freedom, justice and common rights are assumed to be the original, God-given rights of the British. This nostalgic picture relies on myth rather than fact. The reality of postwar life is that the British people have undergone a radical repositioning in terms of national history, class and purpose. It can no longer be assumed that the British are a happy breed, or even that they are comfortable with the idea of a common history that provides them with an effective sense of 'roots' today. Many contemporary Britons feel their country is overrun by migrants, refugees and asylum seekers. Their cities no longer belong to them; their values have been challenged from within and their sense of national destiny has become confused. The overtones of racial superiority and absolutist providence that resound in the annals of British history have been rejected. Yet nothing truly inclusive and solidifying has been devised and introduced to take their place.

For example, consider the phenomenal success of the BBC comedy series, *Little Britain*. The Britain that emerges from this programme is a moronic inferno of welfare state scroungers, terraced-house-dwelling bigots, corrupt leaders, gullible consumers, indignant victims, fat trolls and shrill jobsworths. Insularity, superiority and prejudice reign supreme. British decency and stoicism are presented as opportunities for the amoral and avaricious to gain advantage. The operative word in this Britain is 'little'. The show's creators and stars, Matt Lucas and David Walliams, lead an infantry charge against the dugouts and redoubts of John Bull's landscape and the cradle of his history. If the same guns were turned against ethnic minorities in Britain the accusation of racism would follow in short order, but Lucas and Walliams cleverly avoid this trap. The very title of this callous, funny, scabrous comedy show implies a *bigger* Britain. Interestingly, the shape of this bigger Britain remains elusive and its details are obscure. Yet the outrageous caricatures of British life in the show are only funny because the *auteurs* retain a sense of discerning distance.

If it is right to propose that the contemporary British are riddled with anxieties and doubts about who they are and where they are going, it prompts us to ask who they formerly believed themselves to be and what sense of national direction they had. The answers to these questions do not lie in national conviction or patriotic gore. They lie in history.

# 'Forging the Nation': The Colley Thesis

For the last decade, the primary academic resource in debates about the history of Britishness has been Linda Colley's 1992 book on the emergence of British identity. Her thesis is that British identity was forged in the eighteenth century, not as a spontaneous development, but rather by the state's imposition of 'Britishness' on the hearts, brains and souls of the population. The central vehicles of this epic process of national imprinting were the Protestant faith, the industrial revolution and Empire. All three provided powerful reasons for asserting national unity as the distinctive mark of progress and banishing separatism as backward-looking, primitive logic.

Colley's thesis would be less persuasive if it only relied upon the argument that patriotic nationalism is the product of new opportunities for social mobility, wealth and shared religious conscience. What makes it compelling is her insistence that all of these things – the spread of the Protestant faith, the industrial revolution and the Empire – were ultimately driven by a popular psychology of fear. In the eighteenth century, what might be called 'fear of the Other' became a widespread obsession. Anxieties about cults, conspirators and other ne'er-do-wells inflamed the country. The climax of these fears was the French and Napoleonic Wars between 1793 and 1815. Nothing personified this more sharply than the figure of Napoleon Bonaparte. Although Colley recognizes anti-nationalist traditions of dissent and separatism, she assigns scant significance to them. Instead, she concludes that in the eighteenth century, the British nation-state achieved the feat of transforming the British nation from a chimera (in the sense of being a wild and fanciful creation) into the people's primary social identification and loyalty. The main instrument that accomplished this was fear of the menacing Other.

Many commentators have quibbled with Colley's bold thesis. Some regard it as a conservative reaction to Marxist revisionist history of the 1960s and '70s, especially the work of E. P. Thompson and Christopher

Hill, which placed class struggle at the heart of national history. As such, it is held to exaggerate the eighteenth century's achievement of national unity and underestimate the persistence of class frictions and tensions. Similarly, by focusing on national history after the act of Union in 1707, Colley misses the significance of earlier attempts to forge the nation. In particular, the efforts of Edward I (1239–1307) – who sought to create the first 'Empire' in the British Isles by subduing the Welsh and crushing the Scots (one of his soubriquets was 'the Hammer of the Scots') – and Oliver Cromwell's conquest of Ireland and Scotland during the seventeenth century 'Commonwealth', are absent. These historical episodes both laid the ground for durable alliances between national factions in all four nations and London and sowed the seeds of lasting enmities.

Similarly, trade, marriage and business produced significant integration between the nations before 1707. This is one reason why some Scots saw great advantage from the Act of Union, since it enabled them to participate on equal terms in a much bigger national market. The importance of economic, cultural and social integration before the Act of Union is minimized in Colley's account. Her emphasis upon 1707 produces a misleading binary model of pre- and post-national integration that fails to grasp the multiple, well-trod paths of economic and cultural convergence between the four nations.

Notwithstanding the criticisms, Colley's thesis – that the eighteenth century was the key 'moment' in forging the modern nation – is the main reference point from which serious contemporary debate on British nationalism proceeds.


## Flexible Nationalism: the Rise of the Flexi-Brit

The eighteenth-century proposition that the British are a unified nation, bound together by common blood and shared history, stood in a long line of myths produced among the inhabitants of the British Isles respecting their origins, connections and destiny. As we shall see later, before the Act of Union in 1707 the myths of Albion and Arthur (suggesting a common father and a heroic champion of the people respectively) provided a treasure chest of symbols about who Britons are, where they come from and what their purpose must be. Together with the myth of national unity concocted in 1707 and imprinted upon the population over the next 250 years, these myths were extraordinarily influential. They were the mirror that the British held up to view themselves, and, through the long domination of the British Empire and the role of English as the world's lingua franca, they were how the rest of the world learned to see Britons.

These myths continue to have real consequences for how British people think of themselves and how others regard them in the world today. Their origins lie in the imagination, in fancies of common roots, dreams of solidarity and whimsical notions of common blood. But the contours of national identity that emerged from this disorganized mish-mash were gouged out and reinforced by the state. British national identity was constructed through the state's control, violently wrested from the monarch; of the use of physical force; legislative authority and executive power.

British nationalism involved a particular type of social *inclusion* that is only exposed as singular and exceptional once the issue of what is excluded is articulated. In the words of Corrigan and Sayer in *The Great Arch* (1985):

> Schooling, for instance, comes to stand for education, policing for order, voting for political participation. Fundamental social classifications, like age and gender, are enshrined in law, embedded in institutions, routinized in administrative procedures and symbolized in rituals of state. Certain forms of activity are given the official seal of approval; others are situated beyond the pale. This has cumulative, enormous cultural consequences; for how people identify (in many cases, *have to identify* [emphasis in the original]) themselves and their 'place' in the world.

'Britons' were a pragmatic creation designed to exploit and develop the new economic and militaristic opportunities of expanding trade and industrial, technological and scientific revolution. Religious exceptionalism was used as a tool to legitimize the 'elect' status of the nation (in the sense of being chosen by God).

The main argument of this book is that these myths are no longer binding in an age of mass communication and mass education. Indeed, in a pan-European era, in which ideas and people travel throughout the world faster and more freely than ever before, the eternal, unchanging notion of nationalism is a handicap.

The media response to the National Centre for Social Research findings that only a minority of the population define themselves as British was that British nationalism is in steep decline. However, this is not the only – or necessarily the correct – interpretation of the condition of British nationalism today. If the eighteenth-century state invented British national identity for pragmatic reasons, one could now argue that an increasing number of twenty-first-century Britons are becoming pragmatic in how they position themselves in regard to national identity. To paraphrase a famous passage in Marx, it is now possible to support the British Lions rugby team in the morning, criticize British foreign policy in the Middle East after lunch, and celebrate Edward Elgar and Arthur Benson's patriotic *Land of Hope and Glory* as the quintessence of national identity after dinner. A gap has opened between the representation of the nation and the positioning of the population in relation to 'the nation'. In this gap are emerging a wide variety of flexible, strategic approaches to British national identity. To understand the nature of this transformation, we need to go back to first principles and consider the nature of British roots.

# CHAPTER TWO

# 'Cool Britannia' and the Nation

'Britannia', a Roman name for Britain, appears to have been engendered spontaneously among the people of the British Isles. The Latin rendition is phonetic, as is the Greek, from which it may derive (its origins are obscure). Its first phonetic appearance is in the account of the voyages of the Greek explorer Pytheas of Marseilles in the late fourth century BC. The Greek form is *Prettani* or *Pritani* and can be found in the writings of Polybius in the second century BC and Diodrus and Strabo in the first century BC.

There is a good deal of dispute about what the term means. The weight of opinion rests on the side of the view that it means 'tattooed people'. Yet Caesar's account of the Roman invasion contains little to suggest that tattooing was characteristic of the indigenous people. Instead, he refers to the prevalent use of blue woad, painted not to ornament particular features to emphasize individual difference, but to cover the whole body with a standard insignia or gloss.

It is estimated that the population of the country during the Roman occupation was between two and three million. Roman accounts of native Britons are both amusing and instructive, expressed in the same language of superiority and disdain for the natives that much later generations of British imperialists would use to describe the subjugated peoples of their colonies. For most Roman chroniclers, Britain was not the jewel in the imperial crown. Britons were represented as illiterate, superstitious, polygamous barbarians, garbed in animal pelts or often naked. Strabo claims to have seen British youths in Rome and described them as graceless and bow-legged. Tacitus, whose father-in-law Agricola served with the Roman Army in Britannia, described Britons as varying considerably in physical type, from the red-haired heavily-built people of Caledonia to the swarthy Silures of south-east Wales.

In the writings of both Strabo and Caesar, the people of south-east Britain are portrayed as more advanced in their civilization than the rest of the country. They used a money economy based on the exchange of gold and bronze coins, and exported raw material (gold, silver, iron, grain and hides). However, it would be unwise to read too much into the supposed superiority of the indigenous people in the south-east; the difference between them and the rest of the native population was one of degree. Strabo and Caesar both make it clear that the indigenous people were hopelessly primitive, their rudimentary culture totally inferior to Roman civilization. Moreover, Britannia was never a favoured posting; without the advantages of climate, agriculture and mineral wealth present elsewhere in the Empire, there were little opportunities available to the occupying Roman army for acquiring fortune here.

## The Challenge of the Four Nations

The term 'Britannia' has survived and is used today, albeit most of the time in a rarefied sort of way (although as we shall see, this changed, briefly in the late 1990s), as the poetic term for the nation. It is personified in the shape of the seated female figure, modelled by the redoubtable Frances Stewart, later

Duchess of Richmond, adapting a second-century Roman design on Charles II's Breda medal and copper coinage (1672). The 'Union' shield propped at her side bears the crosses of St George and St Andrew, symbolizing that Britain was a compact of races, each with its separate sense of history, purpose and place, yet each also observant of some kind of connection. In 1797, the trident replaced the spear (generally understood to be a tribute to the maritime exploits of Britain's navy). But – arguably – it was not until eight years later, when Horatio Nelson achieved his victory over the French at the Battle of Trafalgar, that Britons could safely rest assured that Britannia ruled the waves. She became helmeted in 1852, when she appeared on the silver groat, and remains stamped on today's 50 pence coins.

The combination of the flags of St George and St Andrew illustrate the challenge of writing about one nation, the United Kingdom, which is in fact composed of the union of four nations: England, Scotland, Wales and Northern Ireland. In terms of population size, wealth, cultural, political and economic influence, England is by far the dominant partner. Yet there are problems in proposing a 'dominant nation thesis' of the UK which posits that England *defines* the context in which the other three nations function. The United Kingdom is a delicate balance of contradictory elements, legally binding and unwritten conventions and reciprocal under-standings that organize relations between the four nations. Although English dominance is pivotal, it has not resulted in uniform acculturation – Britain is one thing, but England, Scotland, Wales and Northern Ireland are *different*.

A good deal of effort and unresolved angst has been expended by generations of authors on British nationalism over the question of what is left over after account has been taken of the enumerated, distinctive traits of the four nations. This question can be explored at both constitutional and emotional levels. The four nations have made undertakings, often unwritten and resting on convention, with respect to their obligations to each other. In addition, centuries of intermarriage, interbreeding and mixed blood spilled for the British cause has made the relation of each of the four nations to the wider entity of 'Britain' fuzzy. In this book I shall seek to respect the national differences between them. However, I take the view that their shared history makes it pointless to argue that England, Scotland, Wales and Northern Ireland consist of four autonomous elements. One reason for this is that the characteristics and values of each nation in the union have been formed largely through their historical, economic, political and cultural relationships with the other three. The past, present and destiny of the four nations are so intermingled that any attempt to regard them as separate entities would be misleading. Furthermore, viewing the four nations as homogenous is just as unproductive. Among the Scots, there are important historical, economic and cultural divisions between Highlanders and Lowlanders. Scottish metropolitan cultures in Glasgow and Edinburgh define each other as distinctive, and to some degree, mutually antagonistic centres within the Scottish nation. Similar metropolitan rivalry exists between Birmingham, Manchester, Bristol and London in England, and Cardiff and Swansea in Wales. There are also deeply rooted distinctions in Wales between the North and West's Welsh speakers and the more Anglicized population of the south-eastern industrial belt and the Marches (the Anglo-Welsh border country). As for the Irish, religious differences between the indigenous Catholics and Presbyterian settlers from Scotland play a major part in history and contemporary culture. Another important historical distinction here is between the Anglo-Irish landowning aristocracy and the rest of the people.

These distinctions and divisions have produced profound differences in how people think of themselves in relation to blood, place and mutual obligations, and correlate closely to people's strong patriotic identification with the nation and sense of national identity.

Sociological research by Heath, Rothon and Andersen for *Who Feels British?* (2005) found that *ancestry* and *mobility* are crucial factors in determining the level of a personal sense of patriotic identity. Individuals with both parents born in one of the four nations have a stronger sense of national identity than individuals who have a less exclusive national heritage. Similarly, people defining themselves first and foremost as 'British' are more likely to have been more geographically mobile either within or outside the UK, than those who define themselves as English, Scottish, Welsh or Northern Irish.

In writing about Britain, then, the best approach is to think of the four nations as a *configuration* rather than a combination of four separate entities. The term 'configuration' applies to both divisions *between* the four nations that comprise the union and the cultural, social, religious and economic divisions *within* each of them. It implies a delicate state of balance and movement between the four. A move by one group alters the positioning and interrelationships of the others. None is independent, although national rhetoric requires all to think of themselves as such. Nor could one, in achieving constitutional independence from the others, be truly autonomous. For the mixture of history, economics and blood resists political fiat, whether it be expressed in the form of territorial boundaries or constitutional edicts.

As a corollary of this, I propose to break with the intuitive tradition of identifying the nation with essentialism (the attribution of a collection of so-called original or primordial characteristics and traits that define the nation on racial, cultural or social grounds). I contend that there are *no* original or primordial characteristics of the British – nor of the French, Germans, Russians, Poles, Australians, South Africans or indeed any other example of the modern nation state. Native-born Britons were always so interrelated with intruders, be they conquerors, explorers or traders, that they have left behind the notion of the 'original British' in a convoluted history of abandoned births, intermarriage, dispossessed property and migratory pathways. To all intents and purposes this densely entangled past is untraceable, since it commenced before the start of recorded time. Considering oneself an 'original' or 'primordial'

Briton is an affectation born of contemporary British ignorance about history.

I wish to reject a metaphysical notion of what the nation means by defining it in terms of a heart, a soul and other metaphorical 'essences', derived from the motif of the 'body'. Using the analogy of the body to refer to the life of the nation does not compare like with like: nations are not 'bodies', they are combinations of many-sided, conscious and often contradictory interests that come together for strategic purposes and through a sense of nostalgia that often rely upon myths about the shared past that conveniently prevent them from airing their differences and pursuing them. The heart does not pump blood through the brain out of a sense of common purpose, and legs don't walk from a nostalgic sense of what they remember they did yesterday.

Instead, my approach is to examine Britain as a configuration of national relations, bound by the language of national discourse, in which the balance of power between individuals and groups has a long history of change and transition. In this configuration, alongside the Union Jack and the British bulldog, Britannia is arguably one of the central modern symbols representing Britons unto themselves and to the rest of the world over the last 400 years or so. The Duchess of Richmond's portrayal of Britannia constitutes a politicized vision of the nation. It is no longer the coarse descriptive term of Roman times, but a calculated reflection of how its leaders want the nation to be represented, both in the eyes of their fellow countrymen and the eyes of the world. As such, the architects and managers of the nation-state sought to assign a vision of Britain in the world with which many in the nation felt uncomfortable. Britannia aimed to code and theme diverse and contradictory elements in the nation by means of one bold and encompassing symbol. It would not be the last attempt to do so.

# Cool Britannia

'Cool Britannia', a term that originated in the 1990s, refers to the purported renewal of vigour in the lifeblood of the nation. This was not-so-subtly linked with the emergence of New Labour as a credible party of government. As early as 1995, the leader of the opposition and de facto prime-minister-in-waiting Tony Blair began to convene high-profile summits with selected icons of 'young Britain', in order to take readings of the state of the nation. These included Damon Albarn (lead singer of Blur and ambassador of Brit-pop par excellence), and the fashion designer Oswald Boateng. The aim was to identify with figures in British youth

'Cool Britannia': Tony Blair at the opening of Tate Modern, May 2000.

culture that carried international and multi-ethnic prestige, in keeping with the domestic realities of transnationalism and multiculturalism, and the opportunities presented by globalization. This was an exercise in political location and cultural recognition that sought to exploit trends in British pop culture, art, music, fashion, comedy and film and present them as evidence that Britannia was reinventing herself from the crabby dowager of the recent Conservative era. For Blair, it seemed, she now sat flexing in the wings as a cool, contemporary role model, suitable for a generation au fait with a more alluring, modern image of national female British capability, such as, perhaps, the heroic, computer-generated icon Lara Croft. The emphasis on appearance and impression was everything to the Blair government; the key term was 'modern'. The favoured way of conveying this to the British people and the world was *presentation*. In this respect, New Labour was following a well-trodden path, having learned much from the preceding four Conservative administrations.

After eighteen years of Tory rule, Blair and his advisors were intent on presenting New Labour as the tribune for 'modern' Britain. The image of Cool Britannia sought to amalgamate the confidence of traditional national authority on the world stage with the supposed reinvigorated cultural cachet of multi-ethnic, multicultural Britain. As such, it was one of the most striking initial symbols used by New Labour to represent national renaissance. But from what was a renaissance being claimed?

## Thatcherism

The three Thatcher administrations, which commenced in 1979, claimed to revive Britain from its status as the sick man of Europe. When the Conservatives came to power Britain had a low growth economy, inefficient nationalized industries, an innovation deficit in science, technology and management, a state system that was deplored by the right-wing press for perpetuating spongers and idlers and a trade union movement that was dismissed for being out of control. This, they insisted, was transformed into a nation that could now play a full part on the world stage, with a dynamic growth economy equipped with a solid record of economic achievement and shrewd international diplomacy. Voters responded positively to the deregulation and privatization programme, the rhetoric of the law and order society, Euro-scepticism and an authoritarian posture on union power. At the same time, many sections within the nation regarded Thatcher's autocratic style of leadership as imperious, insensitive and divisive. It was a long way from the social engineering and welfare protectionism that ruled national life between 1945 and 1979.

The administration of John Major that replaced Thatcher employed a gentler style of leadership. However, his term of office was buffeted by rough waters in Tory ranks over Europe and increasingly vociferous allegations by the media about political sleaze. The damage had been done. The Conservatives were dismissed for being too close to the Neanderthal prejudices of party members and out of touch with the mood of the country. By the final years of the Tory *imperium* (1979–97), the audience of the faithful for the leader's address at the party national conference seemed to tilt worryingly towards a visible majority of non-telegenic delegates wearing uncool dark glasses, wheelchair-bound or carrying walking sticks, their limbs wrapped in plaster casts, contrasting sharply with the besuited businessmen and career politicians that were pre-eminent in the Thatcher-Major governments. The Tory faithful seemed *old*.

Blair and his advisors were adroit in exploiting and developing this theme. Blair's relative youth was presented as evidence of a break from the once-relevant – but now in many ways senescent – politics of the Old Labour past. Blair's government showed no interest in reviving traditional Labour policies of high income tax and corporatist government in partnership with the trade unions and sympathetic business leaders. Commitment to market solutions was retained in all of the Blair governments, and remained a key note in Gordon Brown's new government. However, it was mixed with a revived acceptance of the state's responsibility to provide a national framework for the successful operation of the market by investment in education, health and other central features of the welfare state. It also recognized that Britain was now a multi-ethnic, multicultural nation from which no retreat was possible. Nowhere was this expressed more sharply than in the zone of culture.

None of the four Conservative administrations showed much concern with this issue beyond its relationship to economics, which was portrayed as the real lifeblood of the nation, and a somewhat cheesy attachment to patriotism, bolstered after the British victory in the Falklands in 1982. Culture and patriotism merged; in Thatcher's view, the industrial/business/military complex made the world go round.

Major modified this somewhat by displaying an endearing populist interest in sport. (Could one imagine the puritanical, work-driven Mrs Thatcher ever asserting avid interest in soccer, rugby, cricket or tennis?) But for Major, culture beyond the Lord's Cricket ground and the Twickenham rugby pitch appeared to be a closed book. Neither Thatcher nor Major recognized youth issues, except when they became a social problem in the form of football hooliganism, AIDS, single teenage mothers or inner-city riots. Neither seemed comfortable with multi-ethnicity or cultural and sub-cultural difference. Their governments were essentially founded upon the principle of rule by the supposed dyed-in-the-wool Anglo-Saxon/Celtic silent majority. The corollary of this was social distance, and a condescending attitude to youth, multi-ethnicity and cultures of criticism.

New Labour recognized that large sections of the public were alienated and divided from the versions of British nationalism espoused by Thatcher and Major. It proclaimed itself to stand for social justice and to respect transnationality; it would commit itself to social inclusion and informal, responsive, transparent government, and also to entrepreneurial innovation and the celebration of cultural difference and vitality. Furthermore, it professed to revere the contributions of women and of multicultural and multi-ethnic Britain. It beheld itself as eager to move beyond the culture of aggressive, narrow Anglo-Saxon/Celtic values and the emotional reserve that were traditionally regarded as the hallmarks of Britishness, and represented as such in the Thatcher-Major years. Yet from the first it enjoined that all citizens must respect common values and standards.

Under Blair, it became *de rigeur* to refer to social responsibility, social inclusion, transparency and efficiency as the modern alternative to the society of self-interest. By publicly associating with representatives of the youth culture aristocracy such as Albarn and Boateng – to say nothing of Princess Diana – Blair unfurled a banner announcing the end of remote, unprincipled government in Britain. Or at least that was how things were designed to appear.

## '60s Redux?

The guest list for the 1997 glitzy election celebration party and Downing Street reception to mark the historic victory of Blair and the New Labour included the alternative comedian Eddie Izzard, the extrovert fashion designer Vivienne Westwood, and the chief songwriter of the Manchester pop band Oasis, Noel Gallagher. Pop groups like Blur, Pulp, Elastica and Oasis, fashion designers like Boateng, John Galliano, Richard James and Timothy Everest, restaurateurs and culinary entrepreneurs like Oliver Peyton and Marco Pierre White, artists such as Damien Hirst, Tracey Emin and art collectors like Charles Saatchi, were fêted for capturing the spirit of Cool Britannia, radiating national confidence, classlessness and turbo-charged international cultural cachet.

Many media commentators were inspired to draw comparisons with Britain in the swinging '60s, when Harold Wilson – the apostle of 'the white hot technological revolution' – was in power. At that time, British culture seemed to be the toast of the world. The Beatles, The Rolling Stones, The Kinks, The Who and a seemingly inexhaustible line of British musicians redefined the parameters of popular music; dramatists such as Harold Pinter, Edward Bond, John Osborne and Joe Orton revolutionized the theatre; painters including David Hockney, Bridget Reilly, Francis Bacon and Peter Blake challenged orthodoxy in the world of art; literary figures like Kingsley Amis, John Fowles, Philip Larkin and Iris Murdoch symbolized the renaissance of English letters; while in film, James Bond epitomized the new British hero.

On the whole, the comparisons made between the mid-1960s and the '90s were untenable and ill judged. Britain in the 1960s was a different nation. Less multicultural and less multi-ethnic, it was also economically poorer; its citizens were more insular and sedentary, insofar as they had less access to mass communications and experience of foreign travel; there was less popular awareness of the health risks associated with poor diet and smoking (both primary and secondary); less than 10 per cent of the population entered higher education, compared with the 40 per cent plus achieved in the '90s; the trade union movement was far more powerful, prompting some political commentators to hold that Britain was a 'corporatist state', ruled by a partnership of elected government leaders, trade union bosses and the chief executives of industrial and financial corporations; McDonald's, Burger King and other global brands were not prominent on the high street; the last remnants of Britain's Empire were being dismantled, while entry into the European Community lay far ahead; and there were only two terrestrial television stations, no satellite broadcast systems and no Internet.

In the 1960s, Britain was still obsessed with its imperial past, independent from Europe, protecting a daunting independent military capacity and affecting equality with the USA and the USSR in shaping world affairs. It was like a wounded divorcée, split from the Empire that gave it the accustomed global buoyancy that it enjoyed between the 1760s and 1930s. It was a nation in denial. The cultural revolution in popular music, literature, television, painting and the other branches of culture revealed the stark absurdity of this position. Peter Cook's famous impersonation in *Beyond The Fringe* (1960) of the genial, doddery Prime Minister, Harold Macmillan, still complacently believing that Britain was at the epicentre of world affairs, exposed brilliantly the hiatus between the world of party politics and the everyday world of popular culture. The Wilson, Heath and Callaghan governments of the 1960s and '70s, went some way to attenuating this by insisting that Britain's national interests lay in the direction of partnership with Europe and promoting diversity rather than protecting class privilege.

Under James Callaghan's term of office, in the late 1970s, the ignominious application to the International Monetary Fund for financial assistance to bail the nation out of economic disaster and the wave of strikes in the public sector in the so-called 'winter of discontent', seemed to signify the need for a redefinition of the nation which acknowledged that Britain was no longer a genuine world power. Unfortunately, the Thatcher and Major governments failed to grasp the nettle by designing a new model of the nation that could get to grips with the realities of globalization, multiculturalism and multi-ethnicity. Instead, they pulled out an ouija board and tried to invoke the spirit of Churchill in the years of World War Two to revive national notions of individualism, bulldog endeavour, purpose and unity. Looking back, it is remarkable how successful this rhetoric was in the 1980s and '90s.

Arguably, the reason for this was not so much incisive politics or a penetrative knowledge of the British people, but simple demography. A large proportion of the population still remembered the national struggles of the 1939–45 war. However, by the early 1990s they were a declining force in the labour market and were dying out as a presence in British life. Nevertheless, invoking the ghost of Churchill proved to be extraordinarily effective in diminishing the force of multicultural and multi-ethnic questions on the national political agenda. But it was also superficial, nostalgic and time-limited. Multiculturalism and multi-ethnicity had changed the face of Britain. This, combined with the free market rhetoric of high Thatcherism, which allowed the voluntary sector to challenge the authority of the state in many areas of national life, altered the rules of the game.

The dismal oscillation between treading water and back-pedalling on questions of multi-ethnicity and multiculturalism that characterized the Major government was really a comment on how fundamentally out of touch Margaret Thatcher was with key transformations in postwar British life – namely ethnicity, sexual preference, ecological consciousness and the position of British people with respect to British history. The Left was also at fault at this time in insisting that class struggle is the central dynamic of life in Britain. What crept up behind the backs of the Tories and the Left in the 1979–97 period was the popular conviction that the history of Britain, especially in the years of Empire, is not necessarily the history that the people of modern Britain would have liked. Insofar as they recognized the issue, Thatcher and Major dealt with it by flag waving and appealing to Churchillian and Victorian values. By the mid-1990s – in fact, as soon as John Major replaced Thatcher as Prime Minister – it was clear to most people that this was not enough.

## Globalization, Multiculturalism and Multi-ethnicity

The challenge facing the Blairite version of Cool Britannia was to define a convincing, new version of British nationalism in the context of pronounced globalization, multiculturalism and multi-ethnicity. These terms are sometimes used rather casually, so it may be as well to be precise about what they mean in the pages of this book.

*Globalization* refers to the penetration of national boundaries by economic, cultural and political international flows of influence and power. It is expedited, reinforced and fundamentally enhanced by several convergent tendencies with respect to the form of the corporation, the shape of technology and increasing global access by international travellers (who might be redefined in twenty-first-century society as the foot-soldiers of globalization).

In the last 30 years, leading business and industrial corporations have become more aggressively global in their economic strategy. They now routinely define their 'domestic' market as the world rather than their country of origin. This means creating a global consumer culture conversant with global brand recognition and investment and marketing strategies that commence with a global rather than a national outlook.

With respect to technology, the rise of the Internet, mobile systems of telecommunications and the growing use of personal computers have created a global network of instant mass communications. News from around the world not only travels faster, it is less subject to national executive power. The Internet offers unprecedented opportunities for global communication and the organization of counter-state social movements.

The expansion of air travel, and the concomitant explosion in numbers of international tourists, has contributed to the breaking down of national barriers. The main beneficiaries have been citizens in the West who enjoy comparatively high per capita incomes. But the trend is global. It would be foolish to propose that international tourism operates in a unilateral way to dismantle national divisions. Global tourism is a source of conflict in some regions where it is claimed that tourists damage the environment and distort the economy. Similarly, in Egypt, Israel, Greece, Kashmir and many other popular destinations, tourists have been targeted for terrorist attacks by groups waging domestic political struggles. Nonetheless, the sheer size of tourist flow in the modern world is unparalleled. Globalization is associated with the acceleration of information, increasing international access and experience. It weakens the hands of states to control information and regulate populations by making national boundaries essentially porous.

Two main versions of globalization theory have emerged. The first emphasizes the standardization and regimentation of global culture that follows the creation and colonization of the global market by multinational corporations. This is akin to the return of mass society and post-industrial society theories of the 1960s and '70s that portrayed the future of the world as some sort of global office in the sky.

The second stresses the interplay of local conditions and global forces. The term *glocalization* has been coined to capture this process. Both versions raise a set of questions that cannot be tackled here. The point to emphasize is that globalization is typically associated with reducing the capacity for manoeuvre of national governments and, conversely, increasing the internationalization of social movements, commerce and communication.

We can illustrate this directly by commenting briefly on leading British brand-names that are in fact owned and managed by foreign companies. The Body Shop is owned by a French company; the British Airports Authority and phone company o$_2$ are owned by Spanish companies; the imperial shipping company P&O is owned by a Dubai-based company; Marconi has been sold to Swedish interests; Harrods is owned by the Egyptian property tycoon Mohammed al-Fayed; Rolls-Royce is German, as are Thames Water and Thomas Cook; Sotheby's, Walkers and HP Sauce are American; the gents' outfitters Gieves & Hawkes is owned by the Hong Kong based company USI Holdings; and Rowntree is Swiss. Some of these companies, notably Harrods, Walkers, Thomas Cook, HP Sauce and Gieves & Hawkes, have cultivated a brand image that is distinctively British. Yet the split between the brand image which associates the product with traits in the nation and the realities of boardroom control illustrates the surprises and tensions that globalization constantly creates.

Since it is no longer tenable to regard nations as economically, culturally or politically independent, it follows that one must stop assuming that the national traits associated with them are in the hands of executive power. Governments can't define national values or traits convincingly any more – in the West, especially in America and the UK, the central values are increasingly defined in terms of abstract values (justice, liberty, democracy) rather than blood and soil.

It is not a question of the multicultural and multi-ethnic mix in the nation. There is a level of disconnection between the history and culture of the nation and the control and representation of the nation. Just as on closer inspection truths about the nation often turn out to be myths, the appearance of what the nation is may often prove to be deceptive.

*Multiculturalism* is the emergence of formal and informal tolerance to different values, politics and lifestyles. The civil rights movement of the 1960s, together with feminism and the gay liberation movement, challenged the precept that national cultures are monolithic. They transformed the national ethos of Western national cultures by inscribing the maxim 'living with difference' as the core principle of modern liberal democracies. Multiculturalism suggests that people do not merely have different identities, but that these identities are positioned in various ways in relation to 'the nation'. The question of how individuals and groups relate to the nation is partly motivated by *flexible* considerations and *strategic* imperatives. The relation between citizens and the nation is not constant or universal. While ubiquitous national rights and responsibilities have been constructed, individuals and groups have latitude to interpret and practice them according to the directives of the culture or religion to which they belong. *Multi-ethnicity* refers to the growth of ethnic communities, distinguished by matters of language, race, religion and colour, within national territories. One in eight Britons is now non-white. They have injected the traditional Anglo-Saxon/Celtic culture with new values of subaltern or independent culture, religion, family systems, cuisine, fashion and business practices. Social scientists now routinely refer to modern British culture as 'hybrid' and national identity as 'hyphenated'. By this they mean that traditional British values of liberty, freedom of thought, fair play, mutual tolerance and justice have accommodated ethnic difference: African-British, Caribbean-British,

Indian-British, Pakistani-British and Chinese-British reside along with the Anglo-Scots, Anglo-Irish and Anglo-Welsh as meaningful categories of 'Britons'.

## Modern Britain: National Facts

The depth of the challenges that globalization, multiculturalism and multi-ethnicity pose for the question of national unity may be illustrated further by examining the composition of modern Britain. In particular, facts relating to the size of the population, its distribution, age profile, mortality rates, ethnic mix, economic divisions and religious composition are important because they constitute the setting in which distinctions of class, gender, subculture and other cultural, social and political forces operate. These facts are sourced mainly from the 2001 Census, available from the Government Statistics website, www.statistics.gov.uk.

## Population: Size, Mortality and Distribution

In 2001 the population of the four nations composing the United Kingdom was 58.8 million. Approximately eight out of ten of them are English. This numerical dominance translates into a greater ratio of economic, cultural and political influence that makes the English the chief partner with Scotland, Wales and Northern Ireland in the union. However, it would be wrong to assume that the three smaller nations are eclipsed by England.

| | |
|---|---|
| England | 50.1 million (80 per cent of population) |
| Scotland | 5.1 million (9 per cent of population) |
| Wales | 2.9 million (5 per cent of population) |
| Northern Ireland | 1.7 million (3 per cent of population) |

The four nations that compose the United Kingdom co-exist in a delicate complex unity involving assimilation, co-operation and the maintenance of independent national identity as well as the pooling of key political and military powers, cultural integration, and economic interdependence. This balance rests on threefold foundations: common respect for the rule of law; shared language; and mutual tolerance. As a consequence, as modern European nation-states go, the United Kingdom contains unusually high levels of diversity in respect of culture, national traditions, legal distinctions, manners and conventions of behaviour.

Life expectancy has increased significantly in the last century. Boys and girls born in 2004 can expect to live for 77 and 81 years respectively. In 1901, the figures were 45 and 49. This brings me to the next key issue about life in Britain today.

## Age Profile

An important general fact about the population of modern Britain is that it is ageing. In 2002 the birth rate reached an all time low. For the first time ever, people aged 60 and over form a larger proportion of the population than children under sixteen. In addition, the number who reach 85 and above is at a record level. This is a result of improvements in diet, healthcare, education, sanitation and the rise in real levels of wealth *per capita*. It means that the over-60s are now the biggest numerical group with access to scarce national resources. They are more likely than younger groups to be property owners and have savings. Furthermore, at the time of writing, changes in European employment law means that the age of retirement is likely to be extended or abolished. These changes mean that the over-60s are likely to have a greater degree of economic and political power in the future than at any time in the history of the nation.

The size of the British population in the postwar period has been comparatively stable. For example, since 1951, the population of Australia has grown by 133 per cent, and that of the USA by 80 per cent. In the European Union, the average is 23 per cent. In the United Kingdom, it has grown by 17 per cent. In 2004, 223,000 more people migrated into Britain than migrated out of the country.

## Ethnic Distribution

The values, institutions and major cities have been irrevocably changed by postwar immigration from the Commonwealth and the emergence of the multi-ethnic nation. Approximately one in nine of the population are of Indian, Black Caribbean, Black African and Bangladeshi descent.

### Ethnic Mix of Modern Britain, 2001

| | |
|---|---|
| White | 54.2 million (92 per cent of UK population) |
| Mixed | 0.7 million (1.2 per cent of UK population) |
| *Asian or Asian British* | |
| Indian | 1.1 million (1.8 per cent of UK population) |
| Pakistani | 0.7 million (1.3 per cent of UK population) |
| Bangladeshi | 0.3 million (0.5 per cent of UK population) |
| Other Asian | 0.2 million (0.4 per cent of UK population) |
| *Black or Black British* | |
| Black Caribbean | 0.6 million (1.0 per cent of UK population) |
| Black African | 0.5 million (0.8 per cent of UK population) |
| Black Other | 0.1 million (0.2 per cent of UK population) |
| *Chinese* | 0.2 million (0.4 per cent of UK population) |
| *Other* | 0.2 million (0.4 per cent of population) |

The distribution of ethnic minorities is concentrated in England, where they make up 9 per cent of the population. In Scotland and Wales they constitute approximately 2 per cent of the population, and 1 per cent in Northern Ireland. They are overwhelmingly based in cities; 45 per cent live in the London area where they comprise 29 per cent of the population. Of the rest, the majority reside in one of four other areas: the West Midlands, the Southeast, the Northwest and Yorkshire and Humberside. So, while multi-ethnicity has produced fundamental changes in British society, its effects are undoubtedly most pronounced in the major urban cities and conurbations.

## Religious Mix

Multi-ethnicity and multiculturalism have produced unparalleled levels of religious diversity in the UK. According to the 2001 Census, Muslims are the largest non-Christian group in the nation. They consist of between 1.6 and 1.8 million citizens. Approximately 38 per cent of those live in London, where they constitute the third largest ethnic minority group, after Jews and Hindus.

Ethnic minorities are also religious minorities. In 2001, 75 per cent of the British population described themselves as belonging to a religion. Of these, seven out of ten reported that they were Christian. Almost three per cent reported that they were Muslim and one per cent as Hindu. Of the remaining religious groups, the largest comprise the Sikhs, the Jews and the Buddhists.

It is perhaps useful to distinguish between strong and weak forms of religious observance. It is estimated that only 7–8 per cent of the Christian population attend regular church service. In Scotland, regular attendance is diminishing, but it remains twice the level for England and Wales. Most of the British population have a weak relationship with religious observance. That is, they regard themselves to be believers, but they are not regular churchgoers, nor do they regularly donate money to the Church. In contrast, the majority of Muslims and Hindus have a strong relation to religious observance. They regularly attend religious worship and their religious belief is an important source of personal and ethnic identity and social inclusion.

Despite the decline in religious observance among British people, the established Church remains a powerful symbolic force in the life of the nation. The Church of England, or Anglican Church, came into existence in 1534. Henry VIII declared himself head of the Church, and ever since, the monarch has held the title of Supreme Governor. It remains a coronation requirement for the monarch to promise to defend the Anglican Church. Heirs to the throne are not allowed to marry anyone who is not a Protestant. Nominally, the monarch appoints a number of senior officials of the Church, including the Archbishop of Canterbury. However, as with so much in the arrangement of the British constitutional monarchy the real power behind the mitre is the Prime Minister, whose recommendations the monarch invariably observes.

## Inequality

According to the 2005 Institute of Fiscal Studies report, the median income per week in Britain is £408 gross. Two-thirds of the population have an income that is below this level. In contrast, the average salary of a Chief Executive in one of the UK's top 200 companies is £37,692 per week. Between 1996 and 2002, the top 1 per cent of income group (600,000 people), increased their share of national wealth from 20 to 23 per cent. The bottom 50 per cent (30 million people) suffered a decline in wealth share from 7 to 5 per cent. For most of the twentieth century, the distribution of wealth in the UK was becoming more equally balanced. It is estimated that in 1911, 1 per cent held 70 per cent of national wealth. By 1938, on the eve of the outbreak of World War Two, this had fallen to 56 per cent; in 1960 it stood at 42 per cent, declining further in the 1980s and '90s to an all time low of 17 per cent in 1991. However, in the last decade, as the figures above suggest, there has been a reversal in this trend with the richest 1 per cent gaining a larger share of wealth. The correlation between wealth and health is well documented: men from poorer backgrounds die 7.5 years before men in the richest 1 per cent of the population.

Gender inequality is still common in the UK, but it is declining. In 2004–5 the gender gap between men and women's median rate of pay was 13 per cent, in favour of men.


## Constitutional System


The nature of constitutional monarchy is impenetrable to many foreigners and a mystery to many British. This is because the complex ceremonial aspects attached to it rest upon convention and tradition rather than written rules. Many Americans still believe that one of the key things that makes America different from the UK is that their own nation is not ruled by a king or queen. But although the monarch is indeed the titular Head of State of the United Kingdom, his or her powers are strictly limited. The King or Queen must accept the advice of the Prime Minister in all matters of government. Of course, the monarch has the right to advise and comment on government policy in the weekly audiences that take place with the Prime Minister. However, in the matter of public proclamations on government policy the monarch is obliged to stay mute. Failure to observe this unwritten ordinance would precipitate a constitutional crisis.

## 'A Very Strange Country'

The late French postmodernist writer Jean Baudrillard once declared that Britain is 'a very strange country (cited in Mike Gane's *Baudrillard Live*, p. 208). So it must seem to many British, as well as non-British citizens. For crucial matters of constitutional rule depend upon centuries of unwritten precedent rather than codified rules or democratic elections. The rules of symbolic inclusion and exclusion are notoriously obscure. The reliance on unstated convention carries over into everyday life. Somehow, British people 'know' their place and are quick to disapprove of an upstart or show-off; they 'understand' how to form a queue and become tetchy with queue jumpers; and they favour laconic, reserved greetings with strangers rather than effusive, 'over-the-top' bear hugs. Public life in the nation seems to be conducted in accordance with an indecipherable code that even the British themselves cannot explain.

In the twilight years of her period of government, Mrs Thatcher was fond of nipping the bud of political ambition at conception among her unfavoured MPs, with the utterance of a single cliché: 'Not one of us.' (Clearly, in every democratically elected, publicly accountable prime minister or president there may lurk a *dauphin* from another era.) There is an unparticularized logic of superiority in Thatcher's notorious phrase. It clearly invokes a political division between the Thatcherite version of neo-liberalism and 'one nation' or 'wet' Conservative traditions. But more than this is implied. It is the 'atmosphere' of a person, the perception of the energy that they radiate, the cut of their jib that is it stake. In relying upon unstated, scarcely tangible, nuanced implication rather than testable evidence and substantiated judgement, it is a typically British way of coding meaning and positioning scarce resources. Why bother giving support to a person who is 'not one of us'? Yet Thatcher's reprise of 'not one of us' grated with many Britons in the 1980s and became a political liability in the 1990s. In a complex unity such as Britain, personal pronouns like 'we' and 'us' must be used with due consideration to the forces of globalization, multiculturalism and multi-ethnicity.

Every nation faces challenges in coming to terms with these forces. In Britain, these difficulties are compounded by the long history of Empire in which many ordinary British people automatically associated British values with progress, justice, mutual tolerance and fair play. Postcolonial Britain is a nation in which these values have come home to roost. They must now be applied in a context in which the nation accepts that today it is composed of 'many nations', marked by distinctions of class, gender, ethnicity, occupation and subculture. Distilling the essence of Britain is tricky. For the term 'essence' implies core values and standards that are shared by all. In postcolonial Britain, in which Muslims and Anglicans recognize the same flag, where gays and lesbians are legally recognized as having rights equal to those of heterosexuals, and where many other matters of cultural, political and economic distinction have attained an unparalleled significance in everyday life, the wisdom of attributing essential national values to the population is highly questionable. We can illustrate the difficulties that face us by addressing in the next chapter the recent debate in Britain on the question of whether a 'national' day celebrating the nation should be inaugurated.

CHAPTER THREE

# Is a 'National Day' Possible in Modern Britain?

The challenge of globalization, multiculturalism and multi-ethnicity to traditional models of the nation may be stated simply. If so much 'difference' is acknowledged within the nation, and economic, military and cultural 'convergence' recognized with other nations, what price national unity? And if larger numbers of citizens acknowledge little or no meaningful unity in the nation, in what sense can it be said to *be* a nation?

Typically, nations are primarily distinguished by their history and culture. But the opportunities for the post-imperial nation to use these resources to weld a new version of national unity are limited. Multi-ethnicity means that the nation consists of large parts of the population that regard themselves and their ancestors as the *victims* of imperial rule. Similarly, multiculturalism gives a credited voice to individuals and groups who were either culturally marginalized or driven underground in the heyday of Empire. The concrete questions are: for what do British gays and lesbians and British Muslims have to thank Empire? How can religious differences be disregarded in favour of a model of modern national unity? Why should people who regard themselves to be distinctive on ethnic, religious, economic and cultural grounds, submit to the collective term 'nation'? In particular, what motive might they have in doing this if examples of institutionalized racism and traditional British values still abound in the nation? If the population recognizes no essence in the nation, or if that essence is somewhat 'fuzzy' (Cohen 1995), is the term wholly procedural, with all of the pragmatic commitment and conditionality that this implies?

Finding plausible, inclusive modern symbols that transcend this history and the myths attached to it is difficult. For example, it might be imagined that symbols expressing the traditional British values of liberty, justice, fair play, moderation, mutual tolerance and free speech offer a solid basis for celebrating national unity. When these citizenship rights have been infringed, as occurred under Margaret Thatcher through the legislation on the Council Tax which was widely regarded as unjust, or Clause 28 which restricted the recognition of gay and lesbian identities (or for that matter when Tony Blair committed British Armed Forces to the illegal invasion of Iraq), they have acted as the basis for mass protests which transcend race, creed, colour and locality. Citizenship rights have been achieved by *concrete* historical struggle. It might be thought that commemorating the historical part that the nation played in building these rights would be readily celebrated as the occasion for reaffirming national unity. But it would be wrong to do so.

Consider the heated debate in 2006 to establish a new 'national day' celebrating 'Britishness'. The suggestion was proposed by Gordon Brown, the then Chancellor of the Exchequer, in a widely reported speech to the annual Fabian Society conference. The question of assigning a national day for the UK points neatly to the dilemmas and sensitivities involved in managing a nation which is in fact composed of four nations, each with some interests in belonging to the wider entity of the UK, but where all have an acute sense of the tolerable limits of assimilation.

The four nations that make up the United Kingdom already have national days: St David's Day (1 March, Wales); St Patrick's Day (17 March,

Northern Ireland and the Republic of Ireland); St George's Day (23 April, England); and St Andrew's Day (30 November, Scotland). Generally, national observance of these days is relaxed and unfussy. Only in Northern Ireland and the Republic of Ireland is St Patrick's Day honoured as an official holiday. In the rest of Britain, there is no equivalent to the huge city parades organized and conducted by the Irish-Americans in US cities. Irish migrants in the UK appear to have adopted the national respect for moderation and understatement and confined the celebration of 17 March to wearing shamrock and a drink in the pub with Irish and British mates.

Gordon Brown's proposal was to create a national day that would bring all four nations together in celebration of the United Kingdom. This is in keeping with New Labour's modernizing ethic. However, as with much else about this ethic it raises more questions than answers about what being British means today. Brown volunteered Armistice Day, November 11, as a day already secure in the public calendar that might be usefully redefined to commemorate not only those slain and injured in World War One and the victory over the reactionary forces of the Kaiser, but the core values of the British people as a whole: individualism, energy, mutual tolerance, a love of liberty, fair play, moderation and justice. However, there are insurmountable hurdles facing this suggestion. Although substantial numbers of non-white Empire troops fought and died for the British cause, World War One is overwhelmingly remembered as a conflict based in the European theatre. Armistice day is not sufficiently inclusive to incorporate contemporary multicultural and multi-ethnic interests.

Public discussion about the proposal inspired the BBC to conduct a poll involving 5,000 people to determine what ordinary British people thought might make a suitable national day. The results were published in the *BBC History Magazine* in May 2006:

## Dates for a British 'National Day'

1. Anniversary of Magna Carta (15 June 1215) 1,334 votes
2. VE day (May 8, 1945) 1,039 votes
3. D-day (6 June 1944) 686 votes
4. Armistice Day (11 November 1918) 568 votes
5. Nelson's victory at Trafalgar (21 October 1805) 524 votes
6. Abolition of slave trade (25 March 1807) 321 votes
7. Napoleon's defeat at Waterloo (18 June 1815) 195 votes
8. Birth of Churchill (30 November 1874) 146 votes
9. Cromwellian Commonwealth established (19 May 1649) 95 votes
10. Reform Act passed (7 June 1832) 94 votes

This only served to highlight the difficulties in identifying a suitable date capable of unifying the whole of the modern nation. All of the dates nominated as potential days of national unity carry problems on multicultural and multi-ethnic grounds. Nelson's victory at Trafalgar and the Duke of Wellington's defeat of Napoleon at Waterloo were crucial episodes in the consolidation of the British Empire. Many British citizens object to Empire because, as we have seen, it is regarded as having been built upon racism and naked economic exploitation. The abolition of slavery was a significant achievement in the history of human rights, but it failed to remove racism from British culture, politics or the labour market. For many, it exposed British hypocrisy in formulating a law that was not consistently applied and did not prevent institutionalized racism. VE-day and D-day are significant in the defeat of fascism, but they contributed to the revival of versions of monolithic nationalism that *formally* included multicultural and multi-ethnic groups yet, at the institutional level, retained traditional prejudices. Winston Churchill, as we shall see, is regarded by many of his contemporary compatriots as the greatest Briton of all time. Yet to honour his birth is to celebrate an enthusiast of Empire and defender of the innate superiority of Anglo-Saxon/Celtic values. Cromwell's Commonwealth was a political revolution that decisively reduced the power of the monarch. But it was a revolution of the landed gentry, who showed little concern for the rights of the working class and those without property. Similarly, the 1832 Reform Act extended the franchise, but it did so on grounds of property and gender, leaving only one in seven adult men with the right to vote.

Most votes were cast in favour of the Magna Carta as the object of a day of national unity. While this was a seminal document in the development of democracy and the rule of law, its relevance as a suitable day for celebrating British national unity is questionable. Most obviously, the Magna Carta was an English incident, preceding the Act of Union by several centuries. Unquestionably, it advanced the interests of the private citizen over the monarch, but limited this on grounds of property to feudal lords. It was an important step in developing civil individual rights, but it fell far short of the citizenship rights that we would recognize today as minimal.

Thus, the difficulties in determining a viable historical date for celebrating the national unity of modern Britain relate largely to the acknowledgement of multicultural and multi-ethnic difference. Basic to this is recognition of different versions of Britishness, articulated along lines of cultural and ethnic *distinction*. It is not just a question of the values of individuals and groups at the periphery of the British nation being acknowledged and respected as now part of the centre. It is also a matter of individuals and groups that have traditionally occupied the centre redefining and repositioning themselves and their values in relation to the new multicultural and multi-ethnic realities of national life. The traditional white population has adopted new types of cuisine, dress, *patois*, music and lifestyle values in response to multicultural and multi-ethnic stimuli. New types of Anglo-Saxon/Celtic Britishness have emerged to challenge more traditional, insular identities. Similarly, multicultural groups and

Crowds on Armistice Day, London, at the end of the Second World War.

ethnic migrants have adapted in their own distinctive ways to relate to indigenous British culture. Yet on all sides individuals and groups have also refused to relinquish occupied territory. Multi-ethnic and multicultural groups are wary about perceived threats to their liberties, and they take pride in their origins; inter-generational distinctions and tensions make a single national day model of Britishness problematic.

For example, the first wave of Asian and Afro-Caribbean migrants tended to regard Britain as the host nation and segregated their communities, their lifestyles and communities. Their British born children developed new forms of 'hyphenated-identities' (Asian-British, Afro-British, Afro-Caribbean-British) that recognize ethnic difference but acknowledge cultural fusion along many fronts of indigenous culture and demand the same rights and entitlements as white British-born citizens (Hall 1992a). The nuances of these new ethnicities vary considerably with respect to the type of root ethnicity involved. Key associated variable factors are family structure, religion and networks in the labour market. Yet if all of these complex distinctions are to be incorporated into ordinary, solidifying models of modern citizenship, the question returns: at what price national unity? The model of Cool Britannia never succeeded in answering that question. At least the issues it raised aired the practical questions relating to unity in modern Britain and captured the public imagination.

## Fighting the Political Ostrich

The long era of Conservative rule between 1979 and 1997 resisted redefining the nation to incorporate multiculturalism and multi-ethnicity and postponed demands for the devolution of power from Westminster to Scotland, Wales and Northern Ireland. Instead, a rhetoric of national unity which drew liberally on the wartime eloquence of Winston Churchill and the rediscovered relevance of 'Victorian values' was reiterated. The superiority of market principles was advocated as the best defence of the values of liberty, justice, free thought, free speech, fair play and respect for private property that defined the nation.

For large sections of the population, this defence was beside the point, failing as it did to address the structural mechanisms that created cultural and ethnic inequality and injustice. This mattered little to a government seeking not to represent a 'one nation' view of Britain but to discard the dependency culture it believed socialism engendered and supported.

In cultural terms, Margaret Thatcher was very like an ostrich, and not just in respect of her deluded view that Britain was still central to world affairs. For example, she seemed genuinely astonished that the 1981 race riots in Brixton and Toxteth could possibly occur on British soil. Her public profile held no place for remorse in shredding the fabric of traditional communities by pursuing aggressive policies of de-industrialization. The Miners' Strike (1984–5) was portrayed as a battle against what she, controversially, referred to as 'the enemy within', again invoking the elusive, damning and extremely divisive distinction between 'us and them'. But this time the resonance is not primarily between the British people and other nations, or multi-ethnic migrants to Britain. It is between the values and beliefs of one section of the native working class and the so-called law-abiding, peaceful majority. This is not so much about Victorian values as Victorian anxieties.

Thatcher conducted herself as if the value of solidarity built around communities of socialism is inherently dangerous to the way of life in modern Britain. It had to be crushed and defeated in a highly public way. She persisted with a monetarist approach to the economy that rejected a Keynesian role for the state in economic management, deregulated the market, privatized nationalized industries and she appeared to be nonplussed about the high levels of unemployment, and social distress, especially in working class communities, that inevitably followed. She rationalized this as the price that the nation must pay to get itself back on its feet after decades of state over-regulation and spineless capitulation to the demands of union bosses. Her model of citizenship prized individual energy and self-reliance above all else. She handled Europe with tongs and spoke of further integration in admonishing terms. She was not a feminist, preferring to believe that adversity is the best test of character for both sexes. For the same reason she mistrusted aristocratic privilege and favoured self-made men in her cabinet. She believed in concepts like national pride and honour. Globalization, multiculturalism and multi-ethnicity were acknowledged but glibly so, and always with the unspoken caveat that ultimately they were required to comply with traditional Anglo-Saxon/Celtic values.

Norman Tebbit, a staunch and trusted member of Thatcher's cabinet, unintentionally encapsulated this outdated, monolithic view of culture perfectly with his notorious 'cricket test'. When asked where non-white British immigrants should place their allegiance, he suggested that a relevant criterion might be to ask them who they supported when the English cricket team played a team against their country of origin or, if British born, the country of origin of their parents. This was not untypical of the ethical politics of the Thatcher era in wrapping a complex set of issues having to do with belonging, diversity and difference in a simple yes or no test of national character.

The 'not one of us' problem was evident along many fronts in the Thatcher years of office. It was apparent in the notorious 'Clause 28' which recognized the rights of homosexuals, but forbade them to proselytize these rights; in the callous dismissal of the views of poll tax protesters who regarded Council Tax legislation as unfair and unjust; in the failure to tackle institutionalized racism; in the benign contempt shown to those who argued for a minimum wage; and the indifference to the question of economic inequality. Under Thatcher, everyone was required to stand on their own feet; the proper business of government was not to plan for social and economic justice, but to maintain the rule of law and create the circumstances in which possessive individualism and competition could flourish.

On succeeding Thatcher in 1990, John Major struggled to restore the traditional 'one nation' model of Conservatism in the country. Outwardly, as befits someone who had experienced huge upward mobility, he talked the talk of social inclusion and opportunity. For example, he was less hawkish about welfare state 'scroungers' and more comfortable with the notion of expanding British involvement in the European Community. Major made classlessness the hallmark of his domestic policy. However, he never initiated the systematic fiscal reform and hard monetary decisions about increasing spending levels in public education, health and welfare necessary to correct the iniquities and injuries of class.

In addition, Major failed to get to grips with the issue of colour. In 1993 the murder of the black teenager Stephen Lawrence at the hands of a gang of white thugs led to Conservative dilly-dallying over the legal process; four years elapsed before a public inquiry into the incident was authorized, culminating in the Macpherson Report (1999). This set out a detailed account of institutionalized racism in Britain. Major's government made gestures to break the mould of racism, notably by encouraging higher numbers of non-white candidates to represent the Tories in local and national elections. Yet these were ultimately insignificant in a sea of white privilege that Major did little to control or rectify. As with the Thatcher era, his government seemed out of touch with multi-ethnic Britain and the large sections of the public for whom the market was by no means automatically favoured as the 'best' solution to social, economic and cultural ills.

New Labour skilfully exploited the national exhaustion with government by inflexible market principles and abrasive nationalism. It committed itself to advancing social enterprise, promoting standards of excellence, acknowledging strength through diversity, enabling devolution and sweeping away outmoded forms of privilege. This was presented not merely as a departure from the era of Conservative domination, but also as a break with Labour's past. Old Labour was tarnished with policies of high taxation, economic mismanagement, misguided support for nationalization and a craven relationship of dependency with the trade union movement. New Labour declared itself to be in favour of open government, accountability, listening to the people and dismantling barriers of inequality associated with class, gender and race. It regarded itself as offering a more caring, informal and relaxed style of government that acknowledged multi-ethnicity, disadvantage and the politics of difference and undertook to initiate positive policies to tackle them.

# CHAPTER FOUR

# The Navel of the Nation

If in 1997 there was scepticism in many quarters that 'Cool Britannia' referred less to a real state of affairs than to an aspiration, New Labour was soon presented with a highly emotional incident that appeared to provide incontrovertible proof that national attitudes had changed for the good. Scarcely three months after Blair's victory, Princess Diana died in a car crash in Paris. The media and the government aired this as more than the loss of a popular, high-profile member of the Royal Family. Crucially, it was presented as the untimely death of a progressive, energetic, glamorous individual who symbolized the sort of 'modern', unstuffy, sensitive, creative, independent spirit that the metaphor of Cool Britannia was designed to encapsulate.

The curious, rather sordid aftermath to her death involved allegations of a conspiracy involving the British Secret Service to eliminate a dissenting voice from the house of Windsor – and someone who was rumoured to be pregnant with the child of Dodi Fayed to boot. For some members of the public, Diana was murdered because she posed a serious threat to the hallowed values of the establishment.

Diana was certainly more adept in handling many aspects of contemporary British media than most of her Royal in-laws. In particular, she seemed light years ahead of the Prince of Wales and the Queen in 'naturally' relating to the public and manipulating the press. Instead of shrinking from painful emotional and political issues, she confronted them, often in a highly visible fashion. Diana mattered because she *connected*. Frequently, her public persona was an unpalatable mix of earth mother and publicity junkie. As details of her private life, involving episodes of bulimia, self-injury and ill-judged extra-marital affairs surfaced, a highly unstable personality was revealed underneath the glittering diadem of Royal protocol. Her swift, violent mood changes, permanent sense of being 'got at' and apparent inability to learn from mistakes, suggested bipolar disturbance or, more controversially, Borderline Personality Disorder (which produces rapid mood swings, a victim mentality, hysterical outbursts and paranoia).

Far from driving a wedge between Diana and the public, these difficulties endeared her to the people. Diana did not flinch from making her vulnerability a public concern. This broke establishment codes and marked her as a dangerous wild card in the Royal circle, capable of exposing the patronage and secrets of the Royals to the merciless lens of the media. Conversely, it humanized her in the eyes of the public, since the travails of her life were acknowledged to bear the regal imprint of common betrayals and ordinary desertions. In death, most of the public probably drew the line at conspiracy theories. Even so, she was overwhelmingly portrayed as the victim of the obsolescent class structure built around British emotional repression and hypocrisy.

Public mourning was vehement and prolonged. Between her death and funeral, a veritable mountain of flowers was laid daily outside the gates of her West London residence, Kensington Palace. The media openly presented her as the casualty of the uncaring, self-absorbed House of Windsor. In particular, Prince Charles and the Duke of Edinburgh were depicted as unempathetic, traditional male pinheads lacking the capacity to identify with her problems and, by implication, with the more relaxed, engaged style of monarchy that she struggled to cultivate. As her funeral cortège pulled out of the grounds of Westminster Abbey, it encountered the most *unBritish* sight of a tearful, multi-ethnic crowd, mostly casually dressed and many strewing flowers in the path of her hearse.

Diana's 'can do' approach contrasted with the unblinking reverence for procedure, rectitude and the stiff upper lip that characterized the approach of the Royals to public affairs. Her death left them apparently dangerously isolated from the image of Cool Britannia, inhabiting instead a derelict landscape of outmoded beliefs in class superiority, ineffable order and consistent regulation of the emotions in public. Outwardly, the confidence and buoyancy of Blair and his cabinet appeared to supply a relevant and 'modern' role model. Blair's judgement in emphasizing Diana's contribution in his 'People's Princess' speech, contrasted sharply with the frigid, emotionally vague, response of Prince Charles to the tragedy.


## 'My Land'

Three years before Blair's election triumph, Dennis Potter, the controversial, terminally ill British TV playwright and screenwriter, gave his final, famous television interview to the television interviewer and pundit Melvyn Bragg. It was a moving broadcast. Potter's curious amalgam of chapel morality, sexual adventurism and nostalgia for the pre-McDonaldized nation produced some of the landmark television drama of the postwar period, notably *Blue Remembered Hills*, *Pennies From Heaven* and *The Singing Detective*. Christened 'Dirty Den' by Rupert Murdoch's *Sun* newspaper, Potter's work asked some searching questions about what it means to be British in the postcolonial nation, and how national integrity can be defended from the twin challenges of commercialization and globalization.

In the interview, Potter revealed himself to be an old-fashioned patriot, albeit one in stark contrast to supremacist, one-race alternatives, like those expressed by right-wing commentators such as Julian Amery, Peregrine Worsthorne and Bill Deeds. Potter remarked to Bragg:

> I love my land. I love England, and when I'm abroad, when I'm ...
> that's one of the things I don't have to do any more, but I
> genuinely feel homesick . . . I mean for an idea, almost, and I've
> always loved my country, but not at the expense, not flags and
> drums and trumpets and billowing Union Jacks and busby
> soldiers and the monarchy and the pomp and circumstance of all
> that, but the real – something about our people that I come from
> and therefore respond to.

Potter felt at 'home' with the Forest of Dean and the immense contradictions fostered by the close community life of chapel, manual labour and village schooling. Although his Oxford education and media career exiled him in many respects from this bucolic background, by making it an object of critical appraisal and distance, he was a reluctant émigré. In his work, and as a man, he was continuously drawn back to the forest. In his first book, *The Glittering Coffin* (1960), he wrote magnificently about the 'forceful', 'individual' dialect of the Forest of Dean – so forceful indeed that he thought of it in terms of 'another language'. This insistence on difference, on refusing to accept official versions of the nation, is a deep characteristic of British individualism that long antedates postwar multi-ethnic migration and the rise of multiculturalism. The theme of 'another Britain', a golden land untainted by corruption, is seminal in British culture. As we shall see in the next chapter, it beckons back to the original recorded myths of Albion and Arthur, in which the indigenous people first struggled to articulate a sense of national identity.

Of course, along with dialect, Potter understood Britain to be composed of distinctive variations of family practices, communal aspiration, love of place, reverence for local history, natural mysteries and regional colour. Yet for someone of Potter's generation, every place in Britain, every region and community that espoused and practiced a degree of difference, was inextricably bound to the 'nation'. This generally unmolested regional variation answered to the spirit of nonconformity in the nation. Potter cherished it as one of the hallmarks of national belonging that made Britain different. This was one reason why he loathed the spread of consumer culture in the nation, which threatened to dissolve locality and nonconformity and replace it with the great shopping mall in the sky. The central tension in Potter's book, articulated long before the rise of Rupert Murdoch (whom Potter despised), was the grinding standardization of locality in Britain. Resisting consumer culture and the Americanization of British life was something that Potter regarded as a central duty for the Labour Party in the 1950s and '60s.

The bilious, brilliant nationalist playwright, John Osborne, anticipated several of these themes, especially in his coruscating drama of national decline, *The Entertainer* (1957). The play focuses on the bravura performance of a fading end-of-the-pier comedian going through the motions of amusing an audience and holding together a theatrical company that he mostly abhors. Every iota of Osborne's lacerating self-hatred and public school sense of honour is mobilized in the drama. Archie Rice, the entertainer, represents traditional British values of individualism, decency and forthright candour. His audience is portrayed as a bunch of trampled, bargain-counter warriors colluding with the slide of the nation into a hypocritical Cold War partnership with America and a brow-beaten future of mindless consumerism. At this time, Osborne, who later moved to the Right, shared with Potter the anxiety of a pulverizing national loss moderated by a defiant commitment to building a 'new Britain'. The identifying characteristics of this new land were nebulous.

Potter was an orthodox chapel socialist, while Osborne was a traditional conservative. Both disapproved of the bureaucratic aspects of welfare state management, mainly on the grounds that it stifled British individualism and nonconformity. Both would have also agreed with the phrase coined by the American sociologist, C. Wright Mills (1958), that the US power elite followed a 'crackpot realism' in the conduct of the Cold War. That is, the arms race against the Soviet Union pitted one enemy against the other, but missed the point that building more nuclear weapons would mean that there would be no winners in the event of them ever being used in conflict.

In common with many Left-wing public intellectuals of the 1950s and early '60s, Osborne and Potter loved the flamboyance and energy of American culture but detested the idea of the Americanization of the world. In both of them there is a nugget of opinion that maintains that it would be preferable if the world still followed British values and the British way of life. Of course, this was not the colonial, supremacist twaddle espoused by Lord Curzon, Cecil Rhodes and other British imperialists of their ilk. Insofar as Osborne and Potter articulated a coherent vision of national revitalization, it focused on the revival of traditional, ordinary, decent Anglo-Saxon/Celtic values and ideals in a post-imperial Age. But the realities of emerging multiculturalism and multi-ethnicity in Britain meant that this response would fall short of what was required.

Pace the Anthony Burgess proposition that forms the epigram of this book, the English pronoun 'my' is every bit as treacherous as 'we'. Potter's 'land', his 'England', was no longer a romantic, green and pleasant place in which the Asian communities of Southall, Leicester and Bradford or the Afro-Caribbean populations of Brixton, Harmondsworth and Toxteth could comfortably nestle like chicks in the same nest. It was 'foreign' to the four British-raised, mostly Leeds-based, Muslim lads who eleven years later would blow themselves to pieces, and kill and maim other passengers on three London underground trains and one bus in the '7/7' bombings of 2005 in protest against British involvement in the occupation of Iraq and in support of Osama Bin Laden's objectives in the terrorist al-Qaeda organization. It was as dimly relevant to multi-ethnic inner city populations in Britain as the novels of Thomas Hardy or the poetry of A. E. Housman. The Britain of Osborne and Potter was drenched in nostalgia. It was introspective, whereas the cultural accent in '90s British youth identity was upon mobility, transnationality and social inclusion.

While the demand for a 'new Britain' made by Osborne and Potter was widely popularized by the media and achieved a good deal of public support, it was essentially a plea for traditional national values to be rediscovered and stripped of the layers of hypocrisy that had accumulated around them during the years of Empire. It did not address the new *material* inequalities constructed around the rise of nascent multi-ethnicity and multiculturalism. Anglo-Asian, Anglo-African, Anglo-Caribbean, gay and lesbian cultures were celebrated, but primarily at the level of rights (i.e. they had a right to exist), rather than at the level of social inclusion which would permit them to be regarded on equal terms with the ethnic Anglo-Saxon/Celtic heterosexual tradition. There was also a tension running throughout the argument of Osborne and Potter. For while they lamented the creation of a world in which popular opinion was constructed by the mass media, their plays could not have had the impact that they achieved without mass communications. Their work raised a series of searching and uncomfortable questions about national identity. But the technophobic element in Osborne and Potter and the nostalgic, almost pastoral vision of Britishness that they entertained, begged the question of finding more fulfilling, democratic ways of using the mass media to enrich daily life in the nation.

The later, New Labour attempt to popularize Cool Britannia as a symbol for the modern nation was more realistic about the challenges of multiculturalism and multi-ethnicity. It sought to include individuals and groups from all sections of modern Britain, not merely through the declaration of abstract rights that narrated belonging, but through the identification of the structural mechanisms that created ethnic and cultural disadvantage and injustice. The Blair government's authorization of self-governing, elected assemblies in Scotland, Wales and Northern Ireland (which devolved real fiscal and legislative powers away from Westminster) was a *concrete* contribution to the recognition of multiculturalism and multi-ethnicity.

At the same time, Cool Britannia might be criticized as a hollow image of new Britain because it failed to convey that the modern nation could no longer be organized around monolithic symbols of collectivity and tradition. There is now so much ethnic, cultural and religious *difference* in modern Britain. This requires the development of a new language with which to address the nation. A central part of this language is the recognition that the commitment of individuals and groups to the nation can no longer be assumed to be automatic and unconditional. In conditions of globalization, multi-ethnicity and multiculturalism, the commitment of individuals and groups to the nation is often pragmatic. Citizenship is a matter of *positioning* and its practice is a question of *life-strategy*. Britons may bear the imprimatur of nationality on their birth certificates and carry it around on their passports. But the kind of Britain to which they belong reflects articulation of various inflections of Britishness and strategic judgements about identity. We must move from a model of the nation organized around the concept of the equal belonging of citizens to a primordial national essence, to a model that acknowledges *determinate belonging*, organized finally on the position of individuals and groups in relation to scarce national economic, cultural and political resources. Needless to say, this raises the problem of exclusion, based on cultural and racial grounds. This problem is indigestible in the context of a national rhetoric of equal belonging. We can illustrate this here by returning for a moment not to the subject of those who occupy the bottom layers in Britain, but one who occupied a niche at the top: Princess Diana.

# Nations do not have Navels

The huge impact of Diana's death caused many British people to experience it as a loss in the *family* of the nation. This was an illusion. 'Nations', as Ernest Gellner once famously remarked in his *Nationalism* (1995), 'do not have navels'. A great many errors derive from using the analogies of family life and kith and kin to refer to the affairs of the nation-state. The mid-eighteenth-century German tradition of conceptualizing culture obscured this. In the writings of Johann Gottfried Herder, *kultur* is presented as the lifeblood of the nation. It is what holds society together. Herder's concept is ideological rather than descriptive, since it sought to act as the catalyst for German unity. It has been the source of a great deal of muddled thinking about the meaning of nations. The idea of lifeblood coursing through the veins of the nation may be instinctively attractive, but it gets analysis off on the wrong foot. National blood ties are always more mixed, loyalties and interests more divided. These tendencies are reinforced in an age of mass communications and mass migration in which, in the West at least, ideas, opinions and people travel more freely than ever before.

In English, the term *nation* entered common currency during the thirteenth century, when it was deployed to refer to a people characterized by common racial affinities. Implicit was a separate meaning of a political group that stands in a relation of representation with respect to the nation. This group includes nationalist movements of various kinds, but its focal point is the nation-state. The nation-state might be defined as the specialized, dedicated body that assumes the task of representing the nation unto its people and to other peoples located outside national boundaries.

Loosely speaking, until the seventeenth century the monarch's court was decisive in playing this role; but after the declaration of the Cromwellian Commonwealth, Parliament and the national institutions created and funded by Parliament became central. The term 'representation' is deliberately wide and encompasses diplomacy, public economic investment in projects of national importance, the state funding of culture, sport and the arts and warfare. By the seventeenth century the term *nation* crystallized to refer to the whole body of the people, in which the nation-state presented itself as acting as a sort of democratically accountable mouthpiece for the nation and the true, legitimate exponent of the ideology of nationalism.

The conceit of presenting the nation-state as the mouthpiece of the nation is a matter of ideology. In the seventeenth century, under the influence of the piratical exploits of Elizabethan explorers, the rhetoric of advancing nationalism bolstered and developed the nation as equivalent to the nation-state. It was an act of fiat imposed by adventurers intent upon presenting national unity and religious superiority as the basis for engaging on military-style incursions into foreign territories. It was encouraged and legitimated by overconfident rulers as the common lore of the nation. It ignored the different positioning of individuals and groups in relation to scarce resources, in favour of a grandstand version of nationalism based on the principle of equal belonging. It was always a myth.

Later, under the British Raj in India, British troops bound for service in the subcontinent were instructed that India was in many ways nothing but a convenient administrative invention. There was no common language, religion or common culture; instead, the 'nation' was a hotchpotch of divided communities affiliated viscerally to ties of locality, regarding wider geopolitical constructions as remote. In short, India was recognized to consist of 'many nations' and colonial success in the colony depended upon understanding this basic fact.

The same might have been said of Britain in the seventeenth century: Gaelic was a different language and the Celtic fringe held fast to beliefs, values and practices alien to most of England. 'Primitive religions' and dissenting traditions stubbornly resisted Protestantism. The 'Glorious Revolution of 1688' brought the Anglo-Dutch monarch, William of Orange and his wife

Mary, to the throne in a so-called 'bloodless revolution'. It revealed how conniving Protestant influence could overcome national prejudice against 'the foreign tongue', and all of the horrors of intrigue and sharp practice associated with it, in favour of a pragmatic solution to the greater spectre of renascent Catholic monarchy. The same would happen in the next century with the coronation of the Duke of Hanover (who scarcely spoke English) as King George I. Regional distinctions between the north, south, east and west, to say nothing of the micro-cultures and economies within these divisions, were significant and obvious to citizens. Individualism, nonconformity and difference were integral to Britishness long before the multi-ethnic influx after World War Two changed the meaning of the nation forever.

## 'Never, come hell or high water'

Prime Minister John Major said as much in his oft-quoted declaration of inalienable, British independence designed to protect the nation from the talons of federal Europe:

> I will never, come hell or high water, let our distinctive British identity be lost in a federal Europe . . . If there are those who have in mind to haul down the Union Jack and fly high the star spangled banner of the United States of Europe, I say to them you misjudge the temper of the British people! . . . And to those who offer us gratuitous advice I remind them of what a thousand years of history should have told them: you cannot bully Britain (*The Guardian*, 10.10.1992)

This speech is now widely derided on account of some key myths about Britain and the British that it reflects and perpetuates. Two in particular merit comment here.

In the first place, Major was wrong to declare that Britain was 'one thousand years old'. In fact, it was less than 300 years old, being the administrative product of the Act of Union (1707) that united the Parliaments of England and Scotland. This was preceded by the union of crowns in 1603, when James VI of Scotland became James I of England. This would appear to have been an appropriate occasion to join the two nations together. But it is a sign of Scottish and, to a lesser extent, English exceptionalism and respect for precedent rather than substance, that nothing of the sort was seriously entertained. Against the wishes of the King, the parliaments of the two nations remained independent until the Act of Union.

For its part, Wales was formally joined to England by the 1536 Act of Union. Welsh resistance to converging with England was never as strong as that of the Scots and Irish. Although the Welsh valued cultural independence, historically they were subdued by the English more effectively than the other two nations that comprise the modern union. In some respects this gave them historical advantages in influencing British politics, especially in the twentieth century, when both Lloyd George and Aneurin Bevan left an indelible Welsh mark on national affairs.

The British like to think of themselves as an ancient race. Actually, in ancient times they were little more than a motley collection of fractious, unruly and often warring tribes of 'tattooed' or 'blue washed people', divided by religion, regional ties, language and culture. The Act of Union with Ireland (1801) established the 'United Kingdom of Great Britain and Ireland'. In 1922, 26 counties of Southern and Western Ireland created the Free State, leaving behind a United Kingdom composed of Great Britain and the six counties of the Province of Ulster, which became formally known as Northern Ireland.

This means that, technically speaking, the United Kingdom is actually younger than the troublesome child that deserted her in 1776: the American colonies. By the same token, technically speaking, the American War of Independence was not fought by the United Kingdom against the

American colonists. Rather it was fought by *Great Britain* – a country that was dissolved in 1801 – and the colonists. However, before we get carried away with this historical, constitutional nicety, we should remember that the United Kingdom did not forget that it had historical interests in America. The UK foolishly endeavoured to regain a foothold in the continent by military means in 1812, only to be defeated by Andrew Jackson at the Battle of New Orleans. Nor was this the end of UK interest in restoring America to what it took to be its rightful place as the child of Britain. Like a long-abandoned father following the actions of his prodigal son, London watched the unfolding of the American Civil War vigilantly, probing and prying for a way to bring the victor back into the fold. What it misunderstood is that Abraham Lincoln regarded the Civil War not merely as the means to quash the separatism of the South, but also as the means of founding the new, industrial American nation-state. For him, a return to the fold was never an issue and only smacked of the unrealistic, sentimental attitudes that the British still nursed about her former colonies.

This means that, to put it bluntly, it is highly misleading to imply that the British are a pedigree family. In reality, they are a mongrel people, formed through an admixture of successive waves of armed Roman, Saxon, Jute and Norman invasions. After the eleventh century, British history is a story of relentless migration. The export of British born ideals, values, prejudices and ways of life was as significant in the construction of national identity as the import of contrasting ethnic and religious traditions. Before the British Empire meant anything as a coherent term, inward migration both enriched and aggravated the people to influences and practices that contrasted with those of the native born.

Until the 1950s, inward migration had little effect on the continuity of national life since most of the immigrants were white Europeans who gradually assimilated almost seamlessly into national life. Mutual tolerance and fair play are often celebrated as two of the classic Anglo-Saxon/Celtic virtues, and in the long history of white migration to the British Isles there is some justice in this. French Huguenots, Italian and Spanish Catholics, German Protestants and Polish Jews redefined themselves as British with comparatively few frictions or tensions. Intermarriage between white ethnic minorities dissolved difference and contributed to the idea that the British are a homogenous race.

However, after the 1950s, Britain began to welcome successive waves of non-white settlers from the former colonies. For reasons of colour, family structure, dress and religion these groups retained a strong sense of separate identity. They were often subject to racism. Their assimilation into Britain was generally more troubled than that of white migrants. Nevertheless, it changed the character of national life. The old assumption of a monolithic island race bound by bloodline and common history ceased to be credible. Although black Britons were an important part of British history, their position in national history was one of deeply rooted categoric disadvantage with respect to national economic, cultural and political resources.

The history of slavery and colonial domination produced a legacy of institutional discrimination. The integration of non-white settlers generated greater friction in British life that flared into the race riots in Brixton and Toxteth in the early 1980s. It also produced unexpected bonuses, such as respect for difference and the assimilation of many multi-ethnic characteristics of lifestyle by the white native population. Multi-ethnicity and multiculturalism changed the ethos of national life by making the culture receptive to the idea of living with difference and loosening the manacles of tradition. By the same token, it required non-white migrants to reach some sort of *modus vivendi* with the idea of British nationality.

Modern Britain is irreversibly multicultural, multi-ethnic and, through media, communication and travel, more porous and susceptible to foreign influence than ever before. The old model of an Anglo-Saxon/Celtic, Protestant, island race, beloved by the twentieth century right-wing Conservative politician Enoch Powell and his ilk, was always a myth. In

British National Party graffiti, 2006.

Powell's day it was a particularly egregious myth, since it crudely labelled non-white settler communities as the main 'threat' to British identity. In the 1960s, Powell made profound errors of judgement on Britain's future. There was unease, tension and violence. But the 'rivers of blood' which he foresaw owed more to his classical education and Greco-Roman fears of the barbarian than late-twentieth-century, multi-ethnic realities in Britain.

Today, the myth of national insularity – which too often has been used as a crutch for espousing British difference – has been fragmented by globalization, multiculturalism, multi-ethnicity and the mass communications revolution. Instant communication via satellite broadcasting and the web and cheap foreign travel combine to integrate Britain indissolubly to the rest of the world by countless visible and invisible population flows and data threads. The idea of British insularity is simply not tenable in the age of Amazon.com and easyJet. Finding the right language to convey this is perhaps one of the biggest challenges facing progressive work on the question of British national identity today.

CHAPTER FIVE

# Myths of Genealogy and Intention

Students of nationalism have grown fond of using Benedict Anderson's 1983 phrase 'imagined community' to refer to nations. It is a good phrase, signifying the attribution of unity and destiny over regionalism, cultural and religious difference. Arguably, it overdoes the metaphor of community for, as we have seen, it is unwise to exaggerate the kith and kin element in nations. A nation is an idea or set of ideas before it is a thing. Because they symbolize belonging and inclusion in unusually cogent ways, myths have always been prominent among the influences that code and theme national life.

The term 'myth' became common currency in English in the nineteenth century. It derives from the Latin term *mythos* and the Greek, *muthos*. Originally, it meant simply a fabulous story or epic tale, usually centred upon a fictitious, idealized person or event, which bestows colour and coherence upon tribal history. Typically, myths of this sort refer to the beginning or dawn of racial or national history. While they were generally understood to be fables, they were nonetheless honoured for revealing something reliable about racial or national character. Like the Arabian tales told by Scheherazade in the *Book of One Thousand and One Nights*, myths were valued as useful fictions that conveyed the essence about a race or nation in ways that history cannot. Because they were densely concerned with origins and lineage, one might refer to them by the term *myths of genealogy*, for they irresistibly suggest the notion of a national 'family' linked together in time and space.

Myths of this type tend to be prominent in the physiognomy of national life. They are stronger in cases where populations have a pure line of ancestry and where geographical mobility is low. Myths are different from legends and allegories because they do not refer to verifiable historical events or social reality. Instead, myths of genealogy are more like fabulous narratives that derive from imagination. They dramatize the culture or world-view of a people, rendering the complex trajectory of history and collective solidarity immediately intelligible through powerful images, bold statements, exotic parables and other motifs. At their most evocative, they capture the relation of the people to their land, vegetation, waters and notable events in history, but transform them into a set of grand 'eternal' codes and themes that automatically provide powerful allegories of national life in the eyes of its people. They take us back to imagined times of paradise – which are, of course, themselves mythical – before the tangled chain of history began to unfold. This is why myths play such a powerful part in the renewal of national life. They provide a paradigm of character at a moment when the components of the nation were less complex and multi-faceted than they are today because, crucially, there was less history on the clock. When history becomes over-complex, or when the people lose their way, a return to foundational myths often provides a sense of renewal based upon coherence and inspiration.

Precisely because they instantly invoke social inclusion and exclusion, myths of genealogy have played a prominent part in the history of migration and conquest. For example, the British puritans who sailed for America in the seventeenth and eighteenth centuries saw themselves as a dissenting, hardy, scrupulously honest, God-fearing family of rugged individualists who defined themselves in opposition to the various styles of discredited European popery and landowning aristocracy. The symbol of a new beginning is always a powerful engine in the creation of myths of genealogy: the settler communities believed that they were embarking on a dramatic new venture in human development that would enable them to build a superior form of society, free from superstition, ignorance, want and the politics of envy. The difficulties of settler life enhanced their identity of social inclusion around notions of racial distinction and Christian solidarity. This integrated the settlers around a shared sense of faith and a common sense of destiny. It also drew sharp lines of opposition between them and native Americans, who were often denounced as savages.

The wider history of European conquest reinforced and intensified this myth by equating civilization and progress with European characteristics and barbarism and superstition with the values, beliefs and lifestyles of the indigenous people of the Americas, Africa and much of Asia. It goes without saying that these myths of genealogy were deployed to legitimize the military-style clearance of indigenous people and the appropriation of native lands, animals and other resources. In this way, myths of genealogy operated as the foundation for the doctrine of European racial superiority. Not only were they used to justify militarism, they underwrote a complex, multi-layered process by which European concepts and values were applied to erase or 'write over' the culture of indigenous peoples. Myths of genealogy function most effectively when they are instantly (without thinking) recognized as equivalent to truth. For much of the imperial era, the doctrine of white racial superiority operated in just this way in the colonized regions of the world.

# British Myths of Genealogy: Albion and Arthur

British national life makes strong appeals to a glorious past. Today, we think of this most readily in relation to Empire, when British global dominance was unparalleled. Yet British imperialists also thought of themselves as walking in the footsteps of giant ancestors. The central motif of myths of genealogy is that the people are singled out and favoured by God. In British myths of genealogy, following Greek, Hellenic and Roman precedents, the original ancestors of the nation are presented either as giant, celestial beings who bridge the divide between the land and the wider cosmos, or supernatural heroes surrounded by an invincible retinue of magicians and spell-makers.

The original figure of Albion was literally portrayed as a giant, who invigorated the narratives on national roots and trajectories written by Milton, the Tudor chronicler Holinshead and William Blake. Albion is actually the oldest recorded name for the island of Britain. Aristotle referred to two large 'Bretannic' islands, Albion (England, Wales and Scotland) and Ierne (Ireland).

Milton and Blake personified this in the figure of the giant of Albion, a member of the Titans (the ancient colossi who once inhabited the primordial Atlantic realm). The Titans were a powerful, but sadly depleted, superannuated race. When the Hellenic tribes overran Greece in the second millennium BC, they installed their sky-god Zeus, and his celestial court at the centre of a new, unifying cosmology. The Greek deities were cast aside and suffered various fates. A significant group became attached to Cronus (whom the Romans later made equivalent to the Italian god Saturn). Cronus had been worshipped as an all-powerful ruler, portrayed as bearing a huge sickle or scimitar which he used to castrate his father. He was honoured by human sacrifice and was believed to have devoured most of his children in order to prevent them from ousting him.

The Titans belong to the world of Cronus. With the rise of Zeus they

Mural of King Arthur's Knights of the Round Table (1895) by Edwin Austin Abbey in Boston Public Library, Massachusetts.

were ejected to the watery frontiers of the Hellenic world. Atlas, who commanded the army of the Titans against Zeus, was transformed into a mountain in what is now Morocco, where he supports the sky on his shoulders. Homer pictures the deposed Cronus and his retinue as banished to a verdant 'Isle of the Blest' where they enjoy carefree immortality. Albion was banished, initially to Provence, and eventually Bretagne. The Druids traced him back to Atlantis, thus creating a direct link between the fabled lost kingdom and Britain. He appears in Spenser's *The Faerie Queene* (IV.xi.16) as

> Mightie Albion, father of the bold
> And warlike people, which the Britainne Islands hold.

Blake appropriated this image and maintained that Albion was the son of Poseidon (the God of the Sea, and himself the son of Cronus and Rhea). In Blake's prophetic writings, Albion's fall and division results in four *Zoas*: *Urizen, Tharmas, Luvah* and *Los/Urthough*. His Albion was therefore the original Briton, the Spenserian 'father of the bold'. This is how he is honoured in British myth today: the great, primordial giant who fathered the people.

The myth of the 'Giant Albion' forms the backcloth to the legend of King Arthur. There are no watertight connections between Albion and Arthur. Nonetheless, intuitively, as the definitive warrior-king of Britain,

Arthur's special powers, epic triumphs and sufferings are often portrayed as descending from the Titans' supernatural gifts.

There is dispute about the real historical existence of Arthur. Evidence of a warrior prince of the fifth century called Arthur exists. He is chronicled in the British poem the *Gododdin* in the ninth century and in the tenth century *Annales Cambriae*. In Geoffrey of Monmouth's, *Historia Regum Britannia* (History of the Kings of Britain), written in the 1130s, Arthur is portrayed as the victor at the Battle of Mount Badon against the Anglo-Saxons, and scourge of the Romans. He is a conqueror who rules over much of Scandinavia and Western Europe and threatens the gates of Rome itself. But he is also the victim of intrigue. After he is betrayed by Mordred and mortally wounded at the Battle of Camlann, he is borne to the Isle of Avalon. Prophecy decrees he will rise again and answer Bretagne's call in her time of need.

However, Geoffrey's source material is dubious. Today, most serious historians argue that it is more realistic to see Arthur as the stuff of the complex interplay of Celtic legend, folklore and mythology which originated with the Welsh and was taken over and embellished by the Cornish and Bretons. It is through this interweaving that the legends of the sword-in-the-stone contest, the creation of the Round Table at Camelot, the quest for the Holy Grail, the tragedy of Guinevere and Lancelot and the throwing away of Excalibur enter the Arthurian tradition.

The Arthurian legend was periodically subject to revival and elaboration in national life. Thomas Malory's *Morte d'Arthur* (1485) was a significant work in this respect, producing a colourful, emulsified history and panorama that added substance to the mystique of Camelot. Malory repeated the prophecy that Arthur will rise again when the nation needs him, thereby portraying the king not only as the country's saviour but also as an eternal, vigilant guardian. In the nineteenth and twentieth centuries these ideas were taken over and elaborated by romantic writers such as Blake, Tennyson, Sir Walter Scott, Rossetti, William Morris, Matthew

Arnold, Mark Twain, John Cowper Powys and T. H. White, so giving Arthur continuity between the dawn of the nation and the present day.

The Arthurian legend was enlisted in the British nation-state formation process. Arthur was a potent symbol of resistance among the Celts of Wales, Cornwall and Brittany, who regarded him as their true sovereign. They cherished hopes that he would return to lead them to expel the Anglo-Norman overlords. This fancy was so powerful and destabilizing that both Henry II and Edward I authorized searches for Arthur's bones to provide evidence that he was dead. Indeed, in 1278 Edward I in his battle to subdue the Welsh exhibited what were purportedly the bones of Arthur and Guinevere. In doing so, he hoped to destroy the myth of a mystic overlord who would come to lead Britons in their hour of need.

The Arthurian cult of chivalry, heroism and romance was adapted by fourteenth century court society. Edward III used Arthurian characters, dress and deeds in the ceremony of the Order of the Garter. There seemed to be a discernible appetite for the fourteenth century court to be connected to the Knights of the Round Table, Camelot and the Vale of Avalon.

In the early modern period the popularity of the Arthurian legend declined. Changes in the organization of politics, war and the economy made the chivalrous ideal less popular. Under the Tudors there was a revival of sorts, symbolized by Henry VII's attempt to bind the Welsh to him by naming his first son after the national hero and making him Prince of Wales in 1489. But, in general, the Arthurian legend receded from prominence in courtly life.

However, in the nineteenth century a dramatic revival occurred in the cult of Arthur. In part, this was a reaction to industrialization, urban blight and the rise of science. Very deliberately, the revival operated with the allegory of a golden age of knights, maidens, minstrels, magicians, sorcerers, gryphons, dragons and unicorns, with Camelot a place of magic and promise. The Celtic West was characterized by authentic chivalry, daring, heroism and romance. It provided a mythical forerunner to

Empire which was itself generally regarded in Victorian and Edwardian Britain to be an inherently noble institution, since it bestowed Christianity, science, trade and industry upon the benighted peoples of the world.

Central to the Arthurian myth are the notions of decay and renewal. The golden age faded, and the Knights of the Round Table disbanded; Arthur was felled by Mordred's treachery, the Grail was lost and the land devastated. Yet in being borne to Avalon, the body of Arthur is transmuted into a misty state of eternal vigilance. The accounts of his mortal wounds are vague and raise questions about his death, and it is unclear where his grave lies; Arthur thus becomes an everlasting life force and the Grail is safely hidden. Some idioms in the legend literally have him waiting in a hollow cave to be called upon by his people in their time of need. Perpetual national renewal is implicit in all of this, and the Victorians and Edwardians drew liberally upon it in representing the imperial quest. The search for the Holy Grail is clearly a metaphor for national struggle and belonging. Arthur's *travails* provide a script for what the nation must endure. His triumphs are the original example of striving and fortitude that the nation must emulate. Camelot will be restored.

Albion and Arthur are myths of genealogy. They do not exactly preoccupy contemporary Britons, but in passing let us note that surely J. K. Rowling has drawn freely on many elements of the Arthurian legend in the successful sequence of Harry Potter books. Similarly, it was surely no accident that the innovative Lancaster bomber that was the backbone of the RAF bombing campaign over Nazi Germany from 1942 was powered by Rolls-Royce Merlin engines. And the public school ethos of honour, daring and chivalry continues to owe much, albeit tacitly, to the assumptions and emotional vernacular of the two myths.

The Arthurian legend is particularly powerful because it seems to reach back to a time of unity, plenty and hope; and is a resource for national renewal in times of trouble and crisis. The reliance of myths of genealogy upon enchantment and magic lifts them from the difficulties of the modern, fractious, rational world wrapped in red tape. They are potent myths symbolizing clarity, purpose and unity.

Albion and Arthur are seminal in the British myths of genealogy because the father figure and the hero are prominent ideas in the repertoire of national narratives. The Victorians greatly approved of Albion because he suggested an unbroken line of succession between Britons and the Ancient Greek Gods. They revived the Arthurian legend because it symbolized a Britain of romance, heroism, nobility and gallantry that could act as a template for the ambitions of Empire. Even today, one can see the association of Arthurian daring, gallantry and courteousness, not only in the ethos of the public schools, but also in the self-image of the British armed forces. Today, these qualities may be themselves regarded as fabulous, horribly distorted narrations in the sight of occupied citizens in Southern Iraq where, at the time of writing, the British Army is policing, often against vigorous native resistance. But it is a powerful element in the self-image of the military and helps to justify their actions. There are strong echoes with the myths of Albion and Arthur and they reinforce the proposition that myths of genealogy have a living presence in the life of the nation.

Nations, then, are inhabited – and in some ways held together – by myths of genealogy. A nation based upon strictly rational principles would have no basis of distinction or differentiation. For, strictly speaking, pure rationality is a universal category and, in principle at least, encompasses all of humankind. Nations are *emotional* categories, in which the emotions tend to outstrip legal-rational principles as the ultimate basis for the attachment of individuals and groups. 'My nation right or wrong' is a familiar position, and one that remains only too evidently a volatile factor in international relations today. But it is an irrational attachment, earthed in myths of genealogy that often have harmful and perverse consequences upon regional and global security.

In confronting the nation, then, we face a force that is both opaque and web-like, as perhaps must be the case when a collection of myths constitute the final banker for a form of collective identity that history constantly belies. When the myths of racial purity and sacred destiny have been unmasked, and the complex cross cutting and hatching of individual and group politics revealed by historiography, the affectation of nationalism stands naked before the world. But despite being recognized as such, it still has the power to mobilize affections, emotions and material resources in support of 'the national cause' – and, of course, against it. This is what makes myths of genealogy both glorious *and* dangerous in the affairs of nations.

## Myths of Intention

In the early nineteenth century, a separate meaning of the term 'myth' emerged. It referred to myths as calculated deceptive inventions designed to confer competitive advantage on individuals and groups. The proponents of these myths recognized their fabulous or false character, and used them deliberately to hoodwink the population. It appeared in parliamentary reports, debates, commissions and enquiries where it was associated with plots or stratagems, usually of a covert nature, intended to present as reliable and trustworthy a picture of reality which was, in fact, selective and false.

Myths of this sort revealed the extension of politics into all areas of everyday life. For example, the myth that the 'underclass' or 'residuum' of city populations was beyond redemption and that 'the national interest' required strong policies of policing and birth control, figured prominently in nineteenth and early twentieth century civic politics and urban planning, health policy and crime control. It represented the intensification of class politics and the designation by middle-class reformers of the underclass as an inherent threat to respectable values. This precipitated a countermovement by progressive elements to initiate an anthropology of

the underclass through which living conditions and ways of life were eluci-
dated and the relationship between these conditions and ways of life and
power were documented. Anthropology and sociology emerged as important counters to urban-industrial mythology and superstition. To be sure,
part of the scientific rhetoric still employed by them is that they dispel
myths; yet they have not succeeded in eradicating myths of intention from
the landscape of contemporary culture and politics.

In the early nineteenth century, this meaning of the term myth was
bolstered from an unlikely source that highlighted the plasticity of reality.
In linguistics, the term myth began to apply to a distortion or 'disease of
the language', as Raymond Williams noted in *Keywords* (1988). Reality
ceased to be understood as an independent objective fact separate from
human consciousness. Instead, it was redefined as the external context of
personal and public life that is fundamentally shaped by language. Since
language was now regarded as constructing the world as opposed to inno-
cently reflecting it, scientific interest began to focus on revealing how
language frames and distorts the shared perception of what we take to be
reality. It was no longer a question of discovering the real world, as if that
world was God-given and existed independently of the tongues of Adam
and Eve. It was now a matter of deciphering the babble of language to
isolate representation from testable propositions of scientific truth.

Myths of this type may be called 'myths of intention'. They can be
distinguished in various ways from myths of genealogy. The latter are
generally unplanned, and arise through the practical attempt of a people to
engage with the land, vegetation, nature in general, the whole ethnic population or to define themselves against other peoples and religions. They are
examples of forms of primitive classification and imagination that seek to
position a people in relation to a physical and social context before the
more refined and complex process of nation-building gets underway. They
help to formulate a sense of origins, and frequently provide an ethos for
claiming national destiny or privilege. In contrast, myths of intention often

directly accompany the nation-building process and arise as individuals and groups struggle to imprint political categories upon society, culture and nature. They are calculated attempts to use manipulation, fable or imaginative distortion to construct a view of reality that underwrites authority and power. Since nation building is a continuous process, myths of intention are fertile sources of calculated distortion usually attached to a political objective or strategy.

Myths of intention are so prolific in the parliamentary system that some analysts regard them as inevitable and, arguably, legitimate parts of modern democracy. This is a sensitive issue. For, formally speaking, democracy is a system of government based on the will of the people wherein questions of truth and reality are publicly debated, rather than imposed by a tyrant or the authoritarian state. Yet because modern democracy is a system in which individuals *represent* the public, the right of deceiving the people is something that senior levels of government appears to exercise when external conditions dictate. Thus, the Conservative cabinet minister William Waldegrave, in giving evidence to the Treasury and Civil Service Committee in 1994, observed that it was sometimes, 'in exceptional circumstances', acceptable to state an untruth to the House of Commons. He referred to the requirement to protect the pound ahead of devaluation as an example of a 'justifiable' lie because it was expressed in the greater interest of national economic stability.

The historical appearance of myths of intention indicated the proliferation of opinions about what the nation exactly constitutes. Of course, in traditional court society there were continuous disputes about the meaning of the nation. Indeed, this was one reason why Charles I was deprived of his head. For his view that the interest of the nation coincides with the interest of the monarch conflicted with the perspective of the gentry, especially in relation to questions of the religious imperative behind monarchy (the idea that the monarch was God's representative on earth) and taxation. But viewed over the long period between Medieval times and

Cromwell's declaration of the Commonwealth, what now seems remarkable is how adept the court was in controlling the debate about national interest and setting an agenda for the nation. In this they were assisted by the absence of an effective national mass communications system and the illiteracy of the majority of the population. This changed with the technology of the printing press, which widened the incentive of ordinary people to become literate and the development of a national system of turnpikes, roads, canals and railways that enhanced connectivity.

What we now call 'the public sphere' – that complex amalgamation of a free press, independent universities, organized and legitimate public opposition (pressure groups, trade unions) – grew rapidly from its eighteenth-century origins in the coffee houses of London, Bristol, Edinburgh and other mercantile centres of Europe and the burgeoning Empire. One may think of it as the market-place of public opinion. Free speech and free ideas could flourish in an ambience that was partly detached from court society.

As the powers of the court waned in favour of the growth of Parliament and representative democracy, persuading the public by winning over the public sphere became the precondition of successful political policy and strategy. Engineering the public sphere – through oratory, advertising and marketing – to support a particular version of 'the national interest' now became a key feature of party politics. This, in turn, reflected the changing balance of power between dominant groups in national affairs.


## Many Nations/National Interests

In the early nineteenth century, the entry into Parliament of representatives from the rising industrial and business classes challenged aristocratic and traditional professional perspectives on the nation. Of course, there was still one Britain, but now many different positions on the nature of

British roots and interests competed for recognition and vindication. The meaning of the nation became contested around class divisions with industry and business challenging aristocratic and professional domination first of all, and, in due course, skilled working class, and eventually, semi-skilled and unskilled versions emerging to lay their own claims on the question. The models of Britain that developed from this interchange over-laid general myths of genealogy, but, crucially, defined themselves from each other in distinctive ways.

For example, the skilled 'aristocracy' of labour sought to create a compelling vision of Britain with the power to inspire and unify, but which at the same time was independent from established aristocratic, business and industrial perspectives, and those of the rising semi-skilled and unskilled strata in the working class. The moves of the middle class to 'reform' society in the 1870s were resented by the aristocracy of labour as an intervention that was not nationally bidden and which failed to heed the newly developing balance of power in British society. In particular, the aristocracy of labour resented the attempts of middle-class reformers to set themselves up as the arbiters of 'respectable society'. This was an important factor in developing the Labour Party, which was regarded by skilled workers as providing a political force to express the opinions and values of those who worked by hand and brain for a living. In other words, the Labour Party began life as not simply a political organization; it was an expression of class *distinction*.

In this context, myths were used not merely to create an atmosphere in which reality and truth were rendered contestable (so that orthodox views of the nation might be challenged legitimately and rising ones articulated). They also allowed sections of the population – positioned differently in relation to scarce economic, social and cultural resources – to assert their presence and prestige on the national stage. In the course of all of this, myths designed to deceive became a central instrument in political struggle.

Facts, half-truths, folk impressions, distortions and falsehoods about the nation were assembled to create a particular atmosphere of public opinion in which calculated definitions of national interest were presented as if they referred to real states of affairs. Through this means, Parliament and the broader public sphere were 'won over' to legitimate party policies and strategies. However, the process of winning over public opinion was always a contingent matter, involving struggle, counteraction and competition. Later generations of social scientists used the term 'hegemony' to refer to this conditional state of affairs in which the power of rule is conceived of as never absolute but always contested.

Of course, it was not the case that myths of this type took over all of politics, driving the struggle for truth into the ditch. There is a noble element in modern politics in which politicians seek to tell the people the truth. Nevertheless, myths of intention (which are designed to persuade by distortion and exaggeration) did emerge as central instruments in the positioning of party politics and the competition for scarce resources.

The meanings of national interest became partly disconnected from the nation, as more and more different groups and parties now entered the fray of public life and waged a struggle to gain hegemonic control. Slowly, the realization took root that not only 'the national interest' but 'the nation' were in part *representations* of reality that reflected the coding and theming powers of rival groups and parties engaged in articulating these qualities to others in the public sphere. National politics remained the art of the possible. However, the role of myths as part of the established repertoire of political deception in conducting the mysteries of this art were relished by the press and later the wider media. Any sentimental idea that democracy separated the modern world from the pre-industrial world of intrigue and thick dissemblance, in which Shakespeare could cheerfully have Richard III confide to his audience that, 'I am determined to prove a villain', evaporated. The press acknowledged myths of intention to be part of the modern politician's tools of trade, and they reported them as such to the public.

# Brit-myths of Intention Since 1982: The Sinking of the *Belgrano*

State strategy and policy continues to use myths of design to win over the population, especially in moments of national crisis. For example, Margaret Thatcher is widely believed to have lied about the sinking of the *Belgrano* in 1982 during the Falklands campaign. The British established a 200-mile exclusion zone around the Falklands and warned that any enemy vessel breaching it faced instant retaliation. The *Belgrano* was torpedoed by the nuclear-powered submarine HMS *Conqueror*, despite not only being outside the exclusion zone but also *sailing away* from its perimeter. Hundreds of Argentinean servicemen lost their lives, and the attack made the escalation of armed conflict inevitable. Critics of Thatcher submitted that she sanctioned the attack cynically to bolster her domestic position and galvanize the nation around the cause of military repossession of the Falklands. This was in the context of her administration's record levels of unpopularity in public opinion polls conducted in the weeks before the Argentinean invasion of the British protectorate. Thatcher gambled that victory in the South Atlantic would overturn this perilous state of affairs and enable her to adopt the mantle of Churchill in articulating national interest. In subsequent interviews, Thatcher has been notoriously evasive about the circumstances of her decision to sink the *Belgrano*. Consistently, she continues to maintain unapologetically that she acted in good faith. The meaning of the term 'good faith' in this context is a matter of conjecture. Myths of intention are contrived to produce an ethos in which facts are manipulated to produce false impressions that either legitimize deception as a part of responsible statecraft, or in which the facts are always presented as inherently hazy and ambiguous.

# Saddam's Iraq

Another notorious example of a recent myth of intention is examined in the Scott Report into the Export of Defence Equipment to Iraq (1996). Sir Richard Scott's inquiry concluded that British ministers in the Major government systematically misled the House of Commons on the question of the sale of British arms to Iraq. The Report is also notable for the manner in which Major's government endeavoured to discredit its findings. On the day of publication, the government issued no less than thirteen press releases from relevant departments in Whitehall contesting Scott's conclusions. The aim was to create a smokescreen of organized, selective misrepresentation of the Report's findings. By this means, it was hoped that the claim of innocence behind ministerial policies would be vindicated. In this case, the Major Cabinet clearly agreed on a version of the national (economic) interest that they judged would be unpalatable if the details were released to the public. So they trimmed, repackaged and remodelled the truth.

The only unforgivable failure in a system of politics organized around myths of intention is for it to be found out. New Labour exploited the reputation of the Major government for deception and sleaze by denouncing the Tories as cynical liars and making large claims about its own integrity and probity. In his first party conference speech on 5 October 1994, Blair made honesty the touchstone of New Labour's approach to government. Pledging that he would strike 'a new contract based on honesty' with the British people, Blair served notice that the recent age of corruption and hypocrisy in politics was moribund. The proof of the pudding would lie in the new politics of candour and honesty that New Labour, he assured people, would apply scrupulously.

The most notorious example of a myth of intention under Blair's leadership was the mendacious gloss put on the allegation that Saddam Hussein's regime in Iraq had significant capacity for biological and chemical weapons of mass destruction (WMD). This was the justification for the illegal war against Iraq led by the Americans and British in 2003. The full extent of Blair's falsehood has been exposed by the Butler Report on Intelligence on Weapons of Mass Destruction (2004) and the Hutton Inquiry into the circumstances surrounding the death of Dr David Kelly (2004).

In the spring of 2002, Blair made a series of statements about 'stockpiles' of Saddam's weapons of mass destruction that the Intelligence Service knew to be inaccurate. Saddam was presented as holding significant biological and chemical capability and on the brink of acquiring nuclear capacity. Blair portrayed Saddam as a tyrant over the Iraqi people, a threat to stability in the Middle East and, through this, a hazard to world peace. These statements were diametrically opposed to the evidence on Iraq's WMD capacity gathered by the Joint Intelligence Committee (JIC) of the day. The JIC reported privately that there was no reliable evidence that Iraq possessed appreciable biological or chemical capacity.

The Butler report and Hutton Inquiry each dwelt on the significant discrepancy between Blair's statements at this time and the knowledge supplied by the Intelligence services. They concluded that Blair's conduct over the allegations concerning Iraq's WMD capacity was misleading on a number of counts. They claimed that his insistence that the Intelligence services were providing cumulative, credible evidence that Iraq's command of WMD was significant, as it was inconsistent with the Intelligence evidence provided to him at the time. His proposition that Iraq was ready to use WMD in the Middle East was at variance with Intelligence assessments that Saddam had no intention of using the small reserves of WMD power at his disposal outside Iraq's borders, unless provoked by foreign attack. In addition, Blair stifled Intelligence warnings that military action against Iraq would significantly increase the exposure of Britain to terrorist attack.

We know that Downing Street actively sought to conceal scientific findings that Iraq possessed no significant WMD capacity. One of the group of experts sent by the UK to investigate the matter, Dr David Kelly, later allegedly committed suicide, supposedly after being suspected of leaking scientific findings concerning the real state of affairs in Iraq to the BBC. This led to the Hutton Inquiry into the circumstances surrounding Dr Kelly's death. The powers of the Hutton Inquiry enabled it to disclose information that would otherwise be protected by the 30-year rule of secrecy that covers official decision making. Through Hutton, we know that the Downing Street Press Office actively sought to reword dossiers from scientific experts that conflicted with Blair's statements that Saddam possessed WMD capability and had plans to use it outside his borders. The Hutton Inquiry also shows that the statement that Blair made in the House of Commons on 4 June 2003, that the Intelligence community supported his view that Saddam had WMD was false.

The real motivation behind Bush's and Blair's decision to invade Iraq is unclear. Perhaps it is incidental that Iraq possesses the second largest proven oil reserves in the world, some 11 per cent of the world's total. Just as the fact that these oil reserves are judged by experts to be of excellent quality and cheap to extract is beside the point (Mann 2005). What is clear now is that the war against Iraq had little to do with Western intelligence that Saddam Hussein's regime possessed significant WMD capability. The truth is that the Intelligence Services found *no* credible evidence that this capability was in place. Bush and Blair chose to disregard the facts and make false claims exaggerating the threat of Saddam's regime to world peace.

The contract of honesty that Blair presented to the British people before his election in 1997 in the self-ordained era of Cool Britannia now reads as if shot though with holes. Is this a consequence of political bad faith? Or does it reveal something of the necessities of representative rule in modern democracy? To put it differently, are myths of intention produced by people with a will to manipulate or do they arise from the challenges of modern democratic politics to achieve more noble objectives of statecraft?

Myths of genealogy and intention are central in creating the ethos in which the nation is constituted and through which citizens recognize ties of belonging and identity with each other. This raises the separate question of how this ethos can be segregated or objectified in order to shed light on what is real or truthful about Britons. How do the British think of themselves? Similarly, how do citizens of other nations see the British? By comparing this data with historical evidence and scientific work on British culture and society, the mythical ethos of British life might be dispelled or at least contained.

This is a tricky undertaking. As the discussion of myth in this chapter has demonstrated, while myths of genealogy and intention are not true, their effects are real in building a sense of what is true about the nation. Myths are so integral to the 'imagined community' of nationhood that disproving them may do little to extricate them from national favour. The next chapter takes up these questions by an analysis of survey material and focus group data on perceptions of the British today.

CHAPTER SIX

# Britons Today

The proposition that myths of genealogy and intention are integral to British nationhood presupposes that it is possible to separate reliable and trustworthy characteristics of Britons from a web of fables and distortions. In a word, it assumes that myths about the British can be *demythologized* to reveal the truth about the nation. Getting to this truth is often a matter of critical historiography. For example, historians have done much to demythologize the Arthurian legend, so much so that the presence of Arthur as a real historical figure in British history is widely discounted.

History can seldom do more than provide a retrospective wisdom about Brit-myth. This may be used to gain valuable insight on national myths today; but while the past informs the present, it does not necessarily reveal much about what the British regard as worthy, admirable, distinctive or reprehensible in respect of national identity today. To acquire this information would require a general social survey and focus group approach that is beyond the budget of most research organizations.

However, some light may be shed by the relatively recent, large-scale survey and focus group material that has come to hand on the questions of how the British see themselves and are viewed by others. This takes the form of a BBC poll conducted in 2002 into the '100 Greatest Britons' of all time, based on responses from 30,000 people. While this data was volunteered freely and cannot be held to represent a scientific cross-section of national opinion, it is an unparalleled statistical resource from the twenty-first century on the question of British national identity. The research prompted a smaller scale survey into the '100 Worst Britons' by Channel 4 (2003) and the 'Ten Worst British Villains of All Time', conducted by the *BBC History Magazine* (2005). Perceptions of British heroes and villains may not be the best test of national character, but insofar as national heroes can be said to embody the most admired characteristics of the people, and villains the least admired traits, they provide a useful gauge of what ordinary British people see as the heights and depths of national character.

By examining this data, we may hope to accomplish two tasks. Firstly, we may separate British views of themselves from myths. Secondly, we may develop insights into the extent to which myths are at the heart of British national identity.

As to the question of how others see the British, useful data are supplied by the MORI poll commissioned by the Royal Society of Arts and published in 2004, involving three international focus groups based in Chicago, Milan, and Mumbai, into perceptions of British values. The poll also interviewed a focus group in Kings Lynn to gain information on how the British see themselves. The research sought to canvas national and international views on distinctive British values. Again, one must enter the caveat that this data does not represent a *scientific* cross-section of British and global opinions about the British. But it has provided some interesting data that may serve as discussion points on domestic and global perceptions of Britons today. Let us examine these findings in turn.

Prime Minister
Winston
Churchill, c. 1942.

## How the British see Themselves: Heroes and Villains

The 2001 BBC poll constitutes a fairly detailed overview of contemporary British perceptions of what is best in the national character. By addressing the subject of the greatest Britons in history, the poll provides an outlook on the wider issue of contemporary British identity – it is reasonable to suppose that what the British admire in their countrymen is also what they would wish to cultivate and practice in their own behaviour. British heroes may be thought of as representing, in exceptional or extraordinary quality, the character traits and values that define the nation as a whole.

The BBC poll defined a 'Briton', somewhat generously, as anyone born in the British Isles, including Ireland, who had placed a significant part in the life of the British Isles. Over one million votes were cast. The results are intriguing.

## Top Ten Great Britons

1   Winston Churchill – 456,498 votes (28.1 per cent)

2   Isambard Kingdom Brunel – 398,526 votes (24.6 per cent)

3   Diana, Princess of Wales – 225,584 votes (13.9 per cent)

4   Charles Darwin – 112,496 votes (6.9 per cent)

5   William Shakespeare – 109,919 votes (6.8 per cent)

6   Isaac Newton – 84,628 votes (5.2 per cent)

7   Queen Elizabeth 1 – 71,928 votes (4.4 per cent)

8   John Lennon – 68,445 votes (4.2 per cent)

9   Horatio Nelson – 49,171 votes (3 per cent)

10   Oliver Cromwell – 45,083 votes (2.8 per cent)

The nation's 'greatest Briton', attracting over 28 per cent of the votes cast, was Winston Churchill. His dominance illustrates an important principle of national identity: national identity is most concentrated when nations face peril. To put it differently, national unity is strongest when it faces a foe.

In Churchill's day, the enemy was of course Hitler's Germany and the associated Axis powers. Churchill's oratorical skills and leadership bolstered national fortitude and resilience during the Battle of Britain. It has a deathless quality because all ranks and sections of the nation were threatened with subjugation and extermination. His eloquent statement of liberty, defiance, justice and resistance exploited and developed traditional British values and redefined them at a juncture when Britain appeared to stand alone in

Western Europe against fascism. British stoicism, endurance and daring were magnified in national culture at this time. Churchill's wartime speeches utilized elements from the adventurist rhetoric of Elizabethan buccaneers like Drake and Raleigh and, of course, the heroic ethos of Empire, dramatized and poeticized by the likes of Tennyson, Henty and Kipling. British singularity in Western Europe in defying Nazi invasion left an enduring mark upon how ordinary British people see themselves, notably in relation to Europe. After all, the principal powers in what is now the European Union were either occupied by the Nazis, or belonged to the Axis alliance. Until the entry of the USA into the fray, Britain stood alone and prevailed.

The strong national self-image of the British standing defiant when other countries on the continent suffered defeat or the ignominy of capitulation became set in stone. This national drama solidified the cultural position of Britons as singular and individual. After all, let us remember that the British broke with the Catholic Church in the sixteenth century; they were the leading partner in the European alliance that defeated Napoleon at the Battle of Waterloo; they were the first industrial nation, and created the most formidable empire in the modern world. All of this has left a bloody-minded streak in the British character that has contributed much to British exceptionalism with respect to the movement towards greater integration in the European Union.

Churchill's popularity underlines the importance that the British attribute to individualism. In researching and writing this book, I have come to think of this as perhaps the defining characteristic of national identity. It is a measure of the huge influence that the USA exerts over global affairs that most people associate individualism with America. But it is the seventeenth-century British political philosopher John Locke, and the deeply rooted nonconformist and dissenting traditions, that crystallized individualism as a core British value.

British individualism owes much to the tradition of common law that emerged from the early feudal period. Common law was independent of the whim of monarchs or the enactments of Parliament. It spoke to an ethic of right and wrong that can only be correctly defined as 'popular', in the sense that its appeal rests in the common usage or spontaneous judgement of the people. It protected the people from those who wished to coerce or direct them. It allowed individualism to prosper because it guaranteed protection to those who sought to differ, providing, as the nineteenth-century political philosopher John Stuart Mill later recognized, that this wish did not interfere with the rights of other individuals.

Incidentally, this is what makes it so challenging to categorize or define the British as a whole. Nationalism suggests unitary, or at least, common traits. But where liberty and individualism are central national values, upheld by a form of justice that is authoritative but largely intangible, it makes for considerable diversity and variation in national types and forms of identity. Postcolonial critics of Empire, such as Paul Gilroy and Stuart Hall, are apt to obscure this point by resorting to a simplistic 'West versus the rest' argument of colonial domination. The thesis not only underestimates the differences between European imperial programmes, but also misses the mixed legacy of colonization.

The top ten contains only two figures born in the twentieth century (Princess Diana and John Lennon). This supports the view that Britain is an 'old country', as Patrick Wright observed in the title of his 1985 book; that is, a nation prone to looking far back into its history for inspiration and mistrustful of modern ideas, architecture and art. The popularity of the fabric and wallpaper designs of Laura Ashley, Terence Conran's interiors, the ersatz ploughman's lunch (actually an invention of brewing companies in the 1970s) and Burberry's vision of British style, balance tradition with modernity. The land and the country house are still celebrated as the cornerstones of national heritage. The elitist public school system and ancient universities continue to be revered by many Britons as the summit of the 'best' education, hallowed by centuries of precedent and worth every penny of the fees levied upon them by headmasters and school governors. Similarly, outside the major cities like London, Manchester, Birmingham and Glasgow, there is deep respect for 'timeless tradition'. The furore over New Labour's ban on fox-hunting with dogs (2004) exposed the strength of feeling, particularly in rural areas, for 'ancient', 'time-worn' ways of life. Similar arguments are made in favour of subsidizing forms of agriculture that are economically inefficient. The 'everlasting' British countryside must be protected against mere market criteria.

The aesthetic resonance of the idea of 'traditional British country life' was sentimentalized and sanctified by William Morris, Thomas Hardy and others in the late nineteenth century. Robert Blatchford, the journalist and publisher of the socialist newspaper *The Clarion*, wrote a famous book in 1893 entitled *Merrie England* in which he advocated the humanizing influence of the arts and the countryside. This vision of the sanctity of the countryside remains extraordinarily powerful in the rural counties. This stress on heritage and tradition does not simply apply to rural spaces and pastimes. In the early 1980s, protecting 'the traditional way of life' of mining communities was presented as an argument in favour of supporting the National Union of Mineworkers. On reflection, it was an odd argument, given the hazards and risks of disease associated with mining life. Yet at the core of it was the common British attitude that fundamentals in the traditional way of life should be preserved.

There is a historical reason for this deep respect for tradition. Apart from the Civil War in the seventeenth century, the notion of armed revolution has been marginal in British life. The Roundheads were Protestant members of the gentry, God-fearing folk whose main aims were to check the power of the King to raise taxes and constrain the power of the Catholics. There were utopian aspects to this war, notably in respect of enshrining individualism, justice and liberty as secular, common principles governed ultimately by Parliament and independent of the jurisdiction of the monarch. But they were always flanked by the pragmatic undertaking to preserve property. Cromwell did not wage the Civil War as a project designed to transform mankind in the manner of the later French and American revolutions of the eighteenth century, or the twentieth century revolutions in Europe and China, fought in the name of Marxism, under the leadership, respectively, of Lenin and Mao. The English Civil War was a clash between two different sets of property interest, one with an allegiance to the King, the other a more democratic formation that stressed the rights of Parliament. It was not an attempt to build a new national order around the rights of the oppressed. Gradualism and compromise have been central to the British programme of nation building. After Oliver Cromwell's death, traditional forces began to reassert themselves, culminating in the restoration of the monarchy under Charles II. But the balance between court and society had been fatefully changed, and Parliament became the decisive chamber for determining the national interest.

What was true of the gentry in the seventeenth century also applied to the workers' movement in the nineteenth and twentieth centuries. Some sections of the establishment were alarmed by the militancy of the new unionism in the 1880s. The successful match-girls industrial action at the Bryant & May factory in 1888, and the London Dockers strike in the following year involving Tom Mann and Will Thorne (self-declared neo-Marxist leaders), were presented as evidence of a rise in working class militancy. Actually, it was nothing but the incorporation of semi-skilled and unskilled workers into traditional models of collective organization that supported Parliamentary representation rather than the overthrow of Parliament. The establishment expressed similar fears over the 'Red Clydeside' (1910–32) group of labour leaders, such as John MacLean, William Gallacher and James Maxton, and also over the General Strike of 1926; but it is untenable to regard either as a genuine revolutionary force. The Red Clydesiders knew their Marx and Engels, and they were accused of sedition by the establishment. But overwhelmingly they followed the traditional path of working class agitation, organization and Parliamentary representation. The General Strike in 1926, involving the so-called 'Triple Alliance' of Railway, Mining and Dockers Unions, was seen by Churchill as a threat to Parliamentary sovereignty; but the strike never galvanized public support and collapsed after nine days.

Between 1940 and 1942, the progress of the Second World War was sufficiently dismal and alarming for George Orwell. In a letter to the *Partisan Review* on 'The British Crisis', to speculate that the British were on the brink of challenging the rule of capitalism. The conduct of the war revealed the injustice and inefficiency of the British system of economic and political power. Orwell regarded Stafford Cripps to be a potential revolutionary leader capable of defying Churchill and the forces of big business. Orwell's letter entertained the dramatic notion that a revolution *within* Britain might take place at the same moment that the country was waging a war against fascism. However, the storming of the Winter Palace was never seriously on the British agenda. The principle of gradualism and piecemeal reform which, with one or two exceptions, has been such a distinctive characteristic of British history, carried the day. All of this contributes to the impression of the British as a people addicted to the ideals of immemorial order and the concomitant hierarchical structure of privilege, rank and deference.

Yet the tradition of gradualism has been so secure in Britain precisely because respect for individualism and justice has been so strong. Common law meant that individualism is an unusually prominent part of British tradition, and with individualism comes dissent and nonconformity.

The BBC poll reflects this. Only one of the top ten was a monarch (Queen Elizabeth I), although both Churchill and Diana were of aristocratic origins. The majority descended from the ranks of ordinary men and women. This respect for achieved power over ascribed (traditional/inherited) power is usually taken as one of the identifying characteristics of modern democracies. As such, it suggests that to emphasize the value of tradition in contemporary British life may exaggerate its significance in

legends and pop idols, only 22 of the top 100 are living; and of those only twelve are from the fields of pop music, film and sport. For every Boy George, David Beckham, Bono or Cliff Richard, there is a Stephen Hawking, Tony Benn or J. K. Rowling. Three out of the top ten are engineers and natural scientists (Isambard Kingdom Brunel, Charles Darwin and Isaac Newton). Indeed, the poll suggests that the British value their scientists above their artists. The British are frequently dismissed as a philistine people, narrowly inured to respect practical knowledge, pragmatism and money-making activities, rather than abstract theory, philosophy and pure research. Yet the BBC poll shows that they value intellectuals, with the caveat that their intellectual labour addresses real world issues. This reinforces the significance of individualism in British national character, and also supports the widespread view that the nation errs towards respect for pragmatism. Of the scientists, Newton and Darwin hardly belong to the great traditions of continental abstract thought. Their work frequently raised abstract issues, but they eschewed questions of phenomenology and existentialism in favour of evidence-based propositions about the real world. Brunel's success in the poll (he gained only 58,000 less votes than Churchill) shows the British respect for ingenuity, energy and practical knowledge. Brunel applied himself to practical problems in various fields of engineering and devised original solutions that revolutionized industrial building and design. This contradicts the earlier stated position that the British are backward-looking and value living in an old country. They also respect innovation, energy and modernity, providing it has a clear, practical bent.

The poll suggests that the belligerent, indomitable quality suggested in the image of the British bulldog is admired by most Britons. Four of the top ten (Elizabeth I, Cromwell, Nelson and Churchill) were noted leaders in time of war. Patently, this reflects the nation's geographical position as an island, vulnerable to sea assault. Elizabeth I and Nelson saved the nation, respectively against the seaborne Spanish Armada and navy of Napoleon

Bonaparte. Churchill did the same, but by air rather than the sea. Cromwell, who was described as 'God's Englishman' in his day, was a more controversial figure. His military policies in Ireland were ruthless, with the massacres at Drogheda and Wexford coming close to genocide. He excused them airily on the arrogant basis that if the Irish could only free themselves from their Catholic priests they might also enjoy the rights of individualism and liberty enjoyed by their English brothers. Yet in leading the rebellion against King Charles I, he displayed the value of English individualism at its boldest and most unflinching.

## Dissent and Nonconformity

The British tradition of dissent and nonconformity has deep roots. It was expressed in the various religious and spiritual groups and movements that developed in reaction to both Catholicism and Protestantism. It continued in the popular reaction against class repression. Shelley gave vent to this in *The Mask of Anarchy*, written in indignation at the 1819 Peterloo Massacre in Manchester when eleven peaceful protesters against hunger and unemployment were hacked down and hundreds injured by mounted yeomanry:

Men of England, heirs of Glory,
Heroes of unwritten story,
Nurslings of one mighty Mother,
Hopes of her, and one another;

Rise like Lions after slumber
In unvanquishable number.
Shake your chains to earth like dew
Which in sleep hath fallen on you –
Ye are many – they are few . . .

Let a vast assembly be,
And with great solemnity
Declare with measured words that ye
Are, as God has made ye, free . . .

*The Mask of Anarchy* is wrongly remembered as a paean to revolution. In fact, it is more conservative in sentiment, being a plea for the *restoration* of the 'natural' or God-given rights of the British advanced by Albion, defended by Arthur and sanctified by the ideal of 'Merrie England'. That it was recognized as such in its day, speaks volumes about the strength of the common law tradition in the land. Common law gave dissenters and nonconformists a greater degree of protection than their counterparts on the Continent enjoyed. The British developed a strong respect for those who spoke their mind, so long as it did not incite violence.

This is evident in the BBC poll. Four of the top ten – Diana, Shakespeare, Lennon and Cromwell – either criticized or opposed the establishment values of their day. Diana's attack on Camilla Parker Bowles, Prince Charles and other members of the Royal Family implied that the probity of the British Establishment was a sham, characterized by presentation and spin, and driven by self-interest.

Shakespeare's historical plays portray the glory of the British, but they also point the finger at monarchical conniving and intrigue. Lennon – the eponymous 'working class hero' – attacked British policies in Northern Ireland, the British class system and British patriarchy. Cromwell dared to participate in a revolution against the Crown and establish himself as the protector of the nation. Respect for dissent and nonconformity echoes the bloody-mindedness of the British.

Further evidence of the strength of the tradition of nonconformity in Britain can be found if one looks beyond the top ten in the BBC poll. Alan Turing, the mathematician, who played a central part in breaking the Nazi Enigma code during World War Two, but was ostracized as a homosexual and committed suicide, is number 21. Emmeline Pankhurst, the leading figure in the Suffragette movement, is 27th. David Bowie, who since the 1960s has challenged artistic and sexual codes, is number 29. Guy Fawkes, the Gunpowder Plot conspirator, is 30th. Thomas Paine, the British revolutionary who penned the inspirational texts *Common Sense* (1776) during the American War of Independence and the *Rights of Man* (1791–2) in reply to Edmund Burke's denunciation of the French Revolution, is number 34. The visionary poet and artist William Blake is 38th. Aneurin Bevan, the Welsh Labour politician responsible for establishing the National Health Service, and who famously denounced the Tory party as 'vermin', is 45th. Boy George, who, like Bowie, challenged aesthetic and sexual codes, is 46th. William Wallace, the Scottish patriot who sought to eject the English from Scotland, is 48th. Freddie Mercury, the camp lead singer of Queen, whose whole life might be interpreted as a rejection of narrow, British masculine conventions, occupies 58th place. James Connolly, one of the Irish revolutionaries who led the 1916 Easter uprising, is 64th. The occultist and drug addict Aleister Crowley is 73rd. Bob Geldof, the pop singer who gained world fame by organizing Live Aid, is 75th. John Lydon ('Johnny Rotten'), the lead singer of the Sex Pistols, is 87th – one place ahead of Montgomery of Alamein. Bono, the lead singer of U2 and activist for world peace, is number 86. Marie Stopes, the campaigner for women's rights who was vilified in her day for advocating birth control, is 100th.

The late Marxist historian, Christopher Hill, entitled his study of John Bunyan *A Turbulent, Seditious and Factious People* (1988). The phrase rings true. The common law tradition in Britain has made the British unafraid of sedition, or to appear turbulent and fractious in the sight of authority. This needs to be stressed, as the deep-rooted strength of gradualism in British history may lead observers to discount dissent and nonconformity too readily. Instead, historically speaking, public life in Britain has a history of more open debate and criticism of authority than prevailed on the

Continent. Of course, this occurred within a context of huge disparities in power between strata. Nonetheless, tolerance for dissent and nonconformity is an important national value in British life, which should never be underestimated in evaluating national character.

## The Worst Britons

The BBC Poll generated great media interest. Inevitably, given the bloody-minded streak in the British, it inspired a counter-blast, focusing on the '100 Worst Britons We Love To Hate' survey, commissioned by the rival television company, Channel 4. This was a less ambitious, and, in truth, rather more trivial and mischievous affair. It involved fewer nominees, drew on a smaller base of votes and the TV programme devoted to it was hosted by the comedian Jimmy Carr.

Interestingly, the top ten figures include six media celebrities (Jordan, Jade Goody, Martin Bashir, Gareth Gates, 'H' from Steps, and Geri Halliwell), which suggests an irascible national attitude towards fame that has been fuelled by the media as a measure of personal worth. Despite the titillation that scandal brings, fame that has been obviously orchestrated by cultural intermediaries, as is the case with Jordan, Jade Goody, Gareth Gates and 'H', or fame that feeds upon publicly exposing the discomfort and torment of others (Bashir's famous interview with Michael Jackson was compelling television but unnervingly cruel), sticks in the craw of the British. This is not a unique trait in Western democracies. Respect for the underdog and the suspicion that the Emperor wears no clothes are hard-won rights of a free electorate. But their prominence in British culture may surprise foreigners used to thinking of Britons as a conservative, docile, obedient people.

Ten Worst Britons We Love To Hate

1 Tony Blair (Prime Minister)
2 Jordan (model)
3 Margaret Thatcher (ex-Prime Minister)
4 Jade Goody (reality TV star)
5 Martin Bashir (TV interviewer)
6 Gareth Gates (pop star)
7 Alex Ferguson (football manager)
8 'H' from Steps (pop star)
9 Geri Halliwell (pop star)
10 The Queen (Head of State)

Bashir's presence is noteworthy. Famous for his revealing interviews with Princess Diana and Michael Jackson, he has attracted disapproval for being over-inquisitive and too swift to find fault. British tact often bewilders and exasperates foreigners, who see it as proof of British indifference and superiority. Actually, it is more accurate to say that it goes with the view that a person's private life is not a matter for public inquiry unless they choose to make it so – either by volunteering public scrutiny or by breaking the laws that govern everyday life. Michael Jackson made this choice with Bashir and there is, perhaps, the public perception that Bashir exploited this trust.

Blair's position at the top of the poll reveals the strong streak of anti-authoritarianism in national character. It is in the nature of the role of Prime Minister of the day to suffer unpopularity. Modern democracies are ethnically diverse and saturated by media opinion; they embrace a wide range of values and consist of increasing numbers of citizens who have experienced higher education and who therefore possess the background knowledge and vocabulary to decode myths of intention. All of this means that no Prime Minister can avoid disapproval. But Blair's unpopularity was intensified by what is widely perceived as a massive default on the promises of open government and transparency that he made upon gaining power. Blair is widely associated with artfulness, guile and broken promises, especially on taxation, student grants, the manipulation of statistics concerning the performance of the National Health Service, state-funded education and, above all, the Iraq War.

The Iraq War was Blair's downfall as a popular leader. It is only with this war that the public associated Blair with outright fraudulence and the perpetration of blatant myths of intention. This perception cast a shadow over the conduct of Blair's tenure at Downing Street. This obscured the progressive policies conducted under his leadership, such as the devolution of power to Scotland, Northern Ireland and Wales; the granting of independence to the Bank of England; the reform of the House of Lords; the creation of a stable economy; the achievement of near-full employment; the reduction of child poverty; the rise in benefit for one-parent families; the halving of the number of pensioners living under the poverty line; and substantial investment in central public services. Blair came to office with high ideals, a modern Hercules ready to cleanse the Augean stable of the Conservative era. It is the perception that he was too ready to abandon and compromise these ideals for the imperatives of *realpolitik* – particularly in preserving 'the special relationship' between Britain and the USA in respect of the unlawful invasion of Iraq – that tarnished his popularity and credibility.

Mrs Thatcher, who occupies third position in the poll, was always a minority leader. Her administrations never achieved more than roughly 40 per cent of the national vote, and her governments were never really about social inclusion. The ideal of the national interest that she popularized was close to the hearts of the traditional middle and working classes. So long as the opposition was fragmented, she could afford to be unpopular with the majority of the country. Indeed, she transformed her unpopularity into a political asset by insisting that the negative reactions of the permissive society, large sections of the working class and many voices in multi-ethnic

Britain, showed that the 'medicine' was working. By driving home the message of individual self-reliance, pride in the nation and scorn for what she regarded as 'bloated' trade union power, Thatcher stirred a hornet's nest of vested interests. In her view, this was justified because these interests were 'responsible' for the low growth/high taxation economy, and a weak version of national identity that she diagnosed as the main cause of Britain's postwar ills.

In *The Hard Road to Renewal* (1988) Stuart Hall coined the apposite term 'authoritarian populism' to refer to a system of rule that is popular among large sections of the electorate, despite manifestly eroding their rights and interests. For Hall, Thatcher's rule was a role model of this. She implemented a series of deep cuts in the welfare state and bolstered the 'law and order' society to the detriment of the working class. Yet many who were adversely affected by these policies backed them as evidence of bold, uncompromising leadership. Vestiges of Thatcher's style of authoritarian populism can be found in Blair's administration, notably in respect of its rhetoric on law and order and criticism of the European Agricultural Policy. But it was delivered in a vocabulary that is more 'reasonable' and appears to set more store in the neo-Christian tradition of compassion and social inclusion. The presence of the Queen at number ten on the list reinforces the view that it is dangerous to view the UK as a traditional, conservative nation. It confirms the continuing power of traditions of dissent and nonconformity in popular culture. The Queen is not especially unpopular compared to monarchs of the last century. She presided over the final dismantling of Empire, and her reign coincided with the rise of multicultural, multi-ethnic Britain in which a new relationship between the people and national identity is still being constructed. Her immediate family reflected many of the personal problems that are widespread among other families in modern Britain. Her sister, Margaret, developed psychological difficulties and was alleged to have developed a dependency on painkillers and alcohol. Three of the Queen's children, Charles, Anne and

Andrew, divorced. Her youngest son, Edward, found it difficult to begin a career. Yet many people, especially those under 50, find it difficult to identify with her or take her seriously as the personification of Britain.

Her *Annus Horribilis* speech delivered to the nation on Christmas Day 1992 reflected on a 'sombre year' that had consisted of a major fire at Windsor Castle, causing £40 million of damage; the separation for divorce between the Duke of York and Sarah; the publication of topless photographs of Sarah with a male pool-side companion in the tabloid press; the Princess Royal's divorce from Mark Phillips; and the separation between the Prince of Wales and Diana. But this was a rare glimpse behind a public face that otherwise has been relentlessly aloof and remote. In contrast with Princess Diana, the Queen has been guarded with her emotions in public. Beyond the values of family and tradition, it is well nigh impossible to know what she believes or values (what for example, is the Queen's position on Third World hunger, abortion, nuclear power, gay marriage, capital punishment and the recreational use of illegal drugs?). As we have seen, it is a requirement of constitutional monarchy that she keeps her own counsel about her values and politics. One consequence of this is that it makes it hard to relate to her on a human level. Today, everyday life is so suffused with political values that political neutrality smacks of abnegation from society rather than the duty to symbolize a majestic force rising above it all for the greater good.

It would be rash to interpret her position at number ten in the poll as a personal judgement delivered by the nation. On the contrary, it reflects the widespread view that remoteness and emotional control are outdated as British traits. As such, it supports the Republican view that constitutional monarchy has had its day and that a more open form of governance is required. Princess Diana was right to submit that the monarchy needs to re-invent itself. The dilemma is how to connect with the people while retaining the status of ascribed superiority. Growing too close to the people destroys the principle of natural superiority, while staying aloof from them raises the question of relevance. Prince Charles and his advisors must feel that they are caught between the devil and the deep blue sea.

In contrast, Jade Goody was a successful contestant on the Reality TV show Big Brother; her presence in the top ten indicates public impatience with figures who are 'famous for being famous'. Jordan makes it to the number two spot probably for her cheerful support of vulgar materialism and her willingness to use cosmetic surgery to further her career. Her ex-boyfriend, Gareth Gates, originally came to fame as the runner up to Will Young in ITV's *Pop Idol* contest of 2002. His version of the Righteous Brothers' 'Unchained Melody' achieved advance sales of 1.3 million and reached number one in the charts. Gates was a pin-up for thousands of teenage girls, but many thought his success was a triumph of spin over talent, and in 2006 his record label Sony BMG chose not to renew his recording contract.

Geri Halliwell is a successful, although declining, singer and former Spice Girl. She has also been a UN Ambassador of Goodwill. Her position at number nine in the poll perhaps reflects distaste among some sectors of the public at her shrill, girl-next-door ponderings about global issues. Some performers, such as Bob Geldof, can switch from the stage of popular music to politics and retain credibility, but Halliwell seemed less relevant in the political sphere, and her involvement was widely perceived as forced and awkward.

Alex Ferguson, the outspoken manager of Manchester United, has probably attracted as many votes from fans of United's rival teams as for his somewhat 'traditional' views about football and man-management. 'H' (for 'Hyperactive') was a member of the band 'Steps' whom voters evidently felt is not as talented as he thinks he is.

In general, the 'Worst Britons' poll demonstrates three things: an impatience with tradition; a mistrust of authority; and a dislike of 'celetoid culture', in which the media create illusory celebrities to fight ratings wars. The strong antipathy to tradition implies that the voters may have been drawn from youth cohorts. There may also be an element of gamesmanship in the poll – Channel 4 presented it as the people's answer to the more sedate, orthodox BBC version that focused on British greatness.

## The Worst British Villains of All Time

By way of counterbalance, the *BBC History Magazine* approached ten leading historians to construct a list of 'The Ten Worst British Villains' of the last 1,000 years. As with the larger BBC poll focusing on all-time British heroes, the *History Magazine* poll was based on the electoral principle that only deceased Britons were eligible. The panel was asked to rank a figure from each century between 1000 and 2000 who would plausibly count as the greatest villain in the century of their birth.

### The Ten Worst British Villains of All Time

| | |
|---|---|
| Oswald Mosley | (1900–2000) |
| Jack the Ripper | (1800–1900) |
| Duke of Cumberland | (1700–1800) |
| Titus Oates | (1600–1700) |
| Sir Richard Rich | (1500–1600) |
| Thomas Arundel | (1400–1500) |
| Hugh Despenser | (1300–1400) |
| King John | (1200–1300) |
| Thomas Beckett | (1100–1200) |
| Eadric Streona | (1000–1100) |

What insights do these figures give us into British character? Oswald Mosley was a flamboyant, aristocratic MP first for the Conservatives and then Labour, before forsaking mainstream politics to found the British Union of Fascists in 1932. He incited anti-Semitism and preached the doctrine of racial purity. His Party received ideological and, almost certainly, financial support from the Nazis. He married his second wife at the home of Hitler's propaganda Minister, Joseph Goebbels. His leadership of the British Union of Fascists positioned him as dictator elect.

Jack the Ripper is a controversial choice, as no one knows who he was, and some theories suggest that he was either American or Polish. Whoever he was, he was responsible for the frenzied murder of at least four prostitutes in Whitechapel, East London in 1888. He continues to haunt the British imagination of depravity and horror.

The Duke of Cumberland's brutal suppression of the Jacobean uprising in 1746 earned him the nickname 'Butcher'; Titus Oates lied about a plot to murder King Charles II which resulted in several innocent people being executed; Sir Richard Rich was a famous dissembler and manipulator, whose evidence against Sir Thomas More and Bishop John Fisher resulted in their execution for treason; Thomas Arundel was Archbishop of Canterbury between 1397 and 1399 and a famous opponent of nonconformity, who used his power to persecute the Lollards; the fourteenth-century courtier Hugh Despenser grew wealthy by eliminating his enemies, but was eventually executed for treason; King John is remembered as a mendacious and ruthless monarch willing to sacrifice all in pursuit of power; Thomas Beckett divided England by engaging in a quarrel with King Henry II over the rights of the Church; and Eadric Streona, King Aethelred II's chief counsellor, was a traitor who helped the Danish King Cnut invade in 1015.

It is fair to say that there is nothing specifically 'British' about this assembly of epic traitors, murderers and intriguers. The behaviour of Despenser, Sir Richard Rich, Streona and King John falls within the range of human guile and manipulation examined by Machiavelli in *The Prince*. The names are different, but the motivations of self-interest and gaining competitive advantage are familiar. Nonetheless, the BBC *History Magazine* poll suggests that arch-villains in British history either betray the nation through espionage or intrigue with enemy powers (Mosley, Streona), or grossly and cynically dismiss the values of tolerance and individualism (the Duke of Cumberland, Oates, Sir Richard Rich, Arundel, King John). The British give short shrift to the argument that politics are dictated by circumstance; instead, they hold fast to national values that transcend time and place. Of these, the three central values are individualism, liberty and tolerance. By no means can the country be said to have a spotless record in applying or protecting these values – many examples of official national policy against the Irish and other colonized peoples and refugees demonstrate that these values have been vitiated. Conversely, it would be rash to underestimate their force in the self-image of Britons or their ideological power in resisting and challenging authoritarianism.

## Exploring 'Britishness'

Holding a looking glass up to the face of the nation may simply reflect self-deception. To get a more balanced picture it is necessary to move beyond national data to examine how others see Britons. A counterweight to the 'Great Britons' poll was provided by the RSA research into how the British are regarded *both* at home and abroad. This was based in interviews with three focus groups based in Milan, Mumbai and Chicago. By way of balance, a British-based focus group was interviewed in King's Lynn. Again, the results are intriguing.

Wit and cleverness were identified as British traits across the board. The Chicago focus group identified politeness and pride as positive attributes of British character, but they also complained that the British are often over-reserved, snooty and have a tendency to be smug and superior. The British were seen as reluctant to display emotion and wary of physical contact like hugging or kissing. Formality defines the British response to strangers. Americans expressed frustration at the length of time most British people take to make real friends. Conformity was identified as a primary characteristic of the British, which is noteworthy given the strength of the tradition of individualism, dissent and nonconformity in the nation. The Chicagoans admired British respect for history, but the Italians regarded this as being a sign of a people shrouded in outdated traditions and customs.

The Mumbai respondents also found a strong thread of superciliousness in British character. They described the British as 'haughty' and arrogant. Britain was criticized for being subservient to American foreign policy interests. The British were congratulated for supporting multiculturalism and showing tolerance to gays and lesbians – but the nation was also regarded as 'the father of racism', and British attitudes to non-white ethnic minorities were held to be ambivalent.

The Italian focus group took a more predictable European line on the British. They described the British as 'isolationist', 'reserved', 'uptight', 'overbearing' and 'snobbish'. The British are seen as bad Europeans who are too often uncritical of America and over-ready to follow America's lead on global geopolitical and economic issues. The Italians saw the British as cold and detached; mindless propriety rather than warmth was regarded to be the British way. For the Italians, propriety often carries over into excessive pride about Britishness and a lack of understanding of conditions in other nations. The Americans criticized the British for the poor state of their teeth, while the Italians dismissed British dress sense and style.

The data contains interesting contradictions. British conformity was universally condemned, but individualism was seen as distinctive of the British. The British are widely regarded as 'remote', yet their sensitivity to gay and lesbian rights is singled out for approval. They are portrayed as a reserved people, yet humour is identified as a key national characteristic.

In short, foreign perceptions of British character seem to rely heavily on a mixture of half-digested historical facts and mythical constructions.

This is not intended as a criticism of foreigners – the same is certainly true of British attitudes towards people from other countries. It reflects the prevalence of visual culture and the image in contemporary popular culture. The image of the British, the Italians, the Americans, the Chinese and so on is the initial resource that people use in coding nations. As we shall see in the next chapter, film and television are crucial in creating and distributing these images.

## Perfidious Albion

Contemporary international impressions are, in some respects, the descendants of much older traditions of international diplomacy and brinkmanship. For example, in the sixteenth-century Spanish allegations about British double-dealing and gamesmanship became pronounced, especially after the defeat of the Spanish Armada. The Napoleonic Wars, which stretched over the end of the eighteenth century and the beginning of the nineteenth century, refined these prejudices against Britain by co-opting the phrase 'Perfidious Albion' to refer to the chicanery and trickery that were held to epitomize the British, from the poem penned in 1793, by Augustin, Marquis of Ximenez. He wrote: '*Attaquons dans ses eaux la perfide Albion*' ('Let us attack the perfidious Albion in her waters'). In 1813, in an example of a prototypal attempt at product marketing, Napoleon Bonaparte used the phrase as the strapline in his army recruitment campaign.

These crude historical stereotypes have remarkable longevity. For example, canards about British 'double-dealing' surfaced during the treaty discussions at Maastricht in 1992 in which John Major and his advisors negotiated the 'subsidiarity' clause. This referred to British opposition to the single currency and the so-called 'Social Chapter' that extended workers' and citizenship rights in the European Union. In effect, subsidiarity protected the British government from federalizing tendencies in Europe that were judged to be inimical to national interest.

Thirteen years later, Tony Blair incensed European opinion and enlarged the popular continental prejudice that the British are bad Europeans, in a different round of budgetary negotiations. In the course of defending the European Union's £4 billion rebate to Britain, he imputed inefficiency and waste to Brussels, pointedly with respect to the Common Agricultural Policy, which provided generous subsidies to the farming community. Blair called for the reform of EU subsidy arrangements and policies. Subsequently, he moderated his position, arguably in response to criticism from the British agricultural industry (a co-beneficiary of the subsidy arrangements). Yet the European prejudice that the British are 'perfidious', and act as if there is one rule for them and another for the rest of the member states, was reinforced.

International perceptions of nations are the victims of encrusted myth and selective history. Often reinforced by historical adventure films and dramas, they ensure that most foreigners relate to other nations through a mixture of stereotypes, historical distortions and national prejudices. This supports a sort of 'automatic' reading of national character that is more direct, but less reliable, than an engagement with the nation and its contra-dictions. When the Mumbai focus group refers to racism and haughtiness as traits of Britons today, it is not clear how much they are influenced by memories of Empire or TV dramas like *The Jewel in the Crown*. When the Milan focus group criticize the British for being 'overbearing' and 'snob-bish', one wonders how far the shadow of military leaders like the Duke of Wellington, or films like *The Winslow Boy* influences them. When the Chicagoans nominate pride and emotional repression as marks of Britons today, one questions if this originates from interaction with real Britons, or contact with representations of Britons through the media and film.

# James Bond and the Politics of Representation

One of the most striking cultural shifts in the last 30 years is the pre-eminence of visual form over literary form. People now respond increasingly to visual data and images more readily than literary texts. Indeed, advertising, film and television are so ubiquitous and seductive that they might be said to supply the common vernacular through which we approach and understand the world. In the representation of national characteristics one can think of popular film as a sort of shorthand, immediately conveying how nations see themselves and are viewed by others. Visual culture works through representation. The image is not necessarily the reflection of what it represents. On the contrary, the image may become detached from what it represents so that our understanding of its meaning is confined with reference to it alone.

Consider the example of James Bond. For many people in the world, Bond is the archetypal modern Briton, displaying the virtues of cool, *savoir faire*, taste and derring-do. At the time of writing, he has figured in 21 films. For many people throughout the world he is the epitome of the eternal British hero, conveying nerve, courage and intelligence. Yet, in reality, he is the product of the 1950s. He consists of a vision of national characteristics calculated by Ian Fleming, the author of the novels, to create a masculine nationalized hero capable of offsetting the trauma of the loss of Empire. Bond's unruffled poise and energetic spirit of adventure, contrasted sharply with the loss of India and the efforts of the postwar Labour government to construct the welfare state around solid bureaucratic principles and dismantle the power of the upper class. As Britain's position as a world power declined, and the cultural advantage in the class struggle moved decisively to the working class, James Bond was invented as a superhero who outwitted both the Americans and the Soviets in the Cold War game. He symbolized a particular argument: British power was waning, and the two Cold War superpowers now controlled the world. But British breeding, experience and style still held the upper hand. In as much as this is the case, Bond became a sort of triumphant echo of Empire.

Bond became a national icon in the 1960s after the release of *Dr No* (1962), just as Beatlemania and interest in British pop culture was becoming a global phenomenon. From the first novel published in 1953, the image of Bond was detached from the reality of British life. The Bond films took over this image and developed it into a code of escapist national fantasy through which Britain was understood by a global audience and through which many Britons regarded themselves. Yet as a national icon Bond was always problematic. His confidence and spirit of luxurious hedonism bordered on a type of arrogance associated with the upper class, from which Ian Fleming hailed.

Harry Palmer, played by Michael Caine in *The Ipcress File* (1965), *Funeral in Berlin* (1966) and the disappointing *Billion Dollar Brain* (1967), was the proletarian spy from South London, invented by the novelist Len Deighton, to provide a 'real world' antidote to the glamorous fantasy of Bond. That he was invented at all shows how much questions of British identity in the twentieth century were negotiated through the aesthetic code of class.

To examine fully how the British have been represented in film, and to trace the full gamut of contradictions between appearances and factual reality, is well beyond the scope of this study. However, in the next chapter a brief examination of how Hollywood represents the British illustrates some wider points about the nation and cinematic stereotypes. The example I have chosen refers to two Mel Gibson period epics that address British values, or rather, what purport to be British values: *Braveheart* (1995) and *The Patriot* (2000).

CHAPTER SEVEN

# The Mel Gibson View of British History

Scotland: AD 1280. William Wallace, the future Scottish patriot, witnesses the brutal slaughter of his father at the hands of the unspeakable English. His foe is the tyrannical, murderous, 'cruel pagan' English monarch, Edward I, (Edward 'Longshanks'). Throughout the film *Braveheart* (1995), the English are portrayed as exulting in terror, torture, pillage and geno- cide; with devil-may-care abandon, they engage in monotonous rape, theft and murder. In contrast, the Scots are presented as amiable, romantic, steadfast, warm-hearted folk, whose warrior class is reluctantly provoked into righteous indignation by the general dastardliness of the English. It is a Manichean plot-line operating on the simple neo-biblical polarity of good versus evil, which suggests the high hand of Hollywood populism at work.

The American-born Australian actor Mel Gibson directed and starred in the film. He invests the role of Wallace with the combination of perma- nently bruised dignity, larrikin whimsy and fateful conscience that are his actorly trademarks. The medieval hanging, drawing and quartering of Wallace at the end of the film is staged as a protracted, heroic martyrdom. Wallace refuses to sup from the phial of poison smuggled into his cell on the eve of his execution by the improbably smitten Isabella, Princess of Wales. Instead, he elects to be tortured and executed for his beleaguered country. Hanged, drawn, castrated, disembowelled and on the point of being beheaded, with his dying breath Wallace still summons up sufficient reserves to bellow a blood-curdling oath of 'Freedom' to the crowd.

The film was fêted as a return to the values of the classic Hollywood adventure yarn, winning Oscars for best picture and best direction. Yet most historians agree that the film is a grotesque travesty of history in which naïve libertarian values have distorted historical character and narrative. Clichéd, eschatological images of English perfidy abound. Edward I, played by the Irish actor Patrick McGoohan, is presented as a cloven-hoofed sadist who abominates the Scots and instructs his archers at the Battle of Falkirk to direct their arrows on the routed enemy with scarcely a moment's remorse for his infantrymen trapped in the crossfire. English yeomen are portrayed more as saps than hearts of oak. Granted, Gibson sides with the English underdog, but in the scenes in which they display fortitude and humanity in the face of the enemy, they are mercilessly reprimanded by their heartless, noble and ultimately indifferent commanders. A sort of class politics is previewed here, in which the downtrodden English are recognized as being in the same position as the colonized Scots, but it is scarcely developed.

Additionally, the old association of English males with homosexuality is wheeled out in the wedding scene of Edward I's son, the future Edward II, to the alluring Isabella of France, played by Sophie Marceau. During the wedding service the boy casts adoring glances at one of his male servants, provoking Edward I into a fit of volcanic fury.

Gibson has Edward I transplant the notorious *ius primae noctis* ('the law of the first night') – the right that permits nobles to exact sexual favours from a serf's bride on the wedding night – to medieval Scotland. The existence of this right, which in medieval France was called *droit de seigneur* (the Lord's Right), is much contested by historians. The evidence that Edward I imposed it upon the Scots is equivocal. As with so much else in his account of the conflict between the English and Scots in the Middle Ages, Gibson does not dwell on historical niceties. His plot requires the English to be villains and the Scots to be victims. So Edward I is presented as implementing *ius primae noctis* as an incentive to attract the priapic English nobility to migrate to the dangerous, turbulent colony. Furthermore, *Braveheart* shows Edward I inflicting a non-representational, punitive system of government upon the Scots, extracting tithes, extending clientism and patronage in every village and town and imposing an inflexible call to arms upon his browbeaten, humiliated subjects.

As a matter of historical record, the romance between Isabella and Wallace is entirely fabricated. Similarly, Edward I is shown on his deathbed rejoicing at Wallace's brutal torture in Smithfield. Yet Edward actually died in 1307, two years *after* Wallace was put to death.

Historians present Edward I as a decisive leader, but one who observed a greater sense of justice and reform than *Braveheart* suggests. His reign is generally divided into two periods. Between 1272 until the early 1290s, Edward is generally recognized to have been an effective military commander and administrator. He acknowledged the need for Parliament and introduced a range of reforming statutes. The escalating financial problems that beset his reign after the early 1290s coincided with domestic frictions provoked by wars with the French and Scots. Edward became more bellicose and intent upon conquest; his tomb bears the epitaph 'Hammer of the Scots'. There can be little doubt that he was a forceful and, at times, cruel war leader, determined to impose the royal prerogative over the people of the British Isles by creating the *first British Empire* over the domestic mainland and islands and crushing claims of national independence. But he also acted as a responsible arbitrator between the claimants to the Scottish throne from 1291 to 1292, and sought to extend the rule of law, albeit on the understanding that he would be accepted ultimately as ruler of the entire kingdom. In many ways his behaviour was typical of the

Mel Gibson as Wallace in *Braveheart* (1994).

European warrior class, chivalric power-broking codes of his day and the Christian devotion to the Crusades.

The film does not convey any of the frictions or tensions within English ranks. Edward 1's England was far from being the green and pleasant land inhabited by an obedient nationalist population speaking with one heart and one mind. Edward defeated the forces of the baronial movement for reform, led by Simon de Montfort, Earl of Leicester, at the Battle of Evesham in 1265. It was Edward's appreciation of the legitimacy of his baron's demands for autonomy that marked the progressive statute building during the first phase of his reign. Medieval society was beset with stresses regarding nationalism, religion and politics. There were vast differences in custom as reflects a country with no effective coast-to-coast system of communications, legal or fiscal framework. At this time 'England' was an incoherent patronym, one that was variously defined and disputed in the regions. Even then, as now, there were many Englands, just as later there were to be many Britains. Individualism and pluralism are the English and British condition; and this is a curse for any writer that wishes to write about them in collective terms.

None of this emerges in *Braveheart*, save perhaps in the execution scene in which Wallace's agonies shame the crowd into sympathy, and spur them to berate his torturers. Even here, the plot never rises above a clichéd battle between good (the Scots) and evil (the English).

The Scots are portrayed in a positive and flattering light, as the simplistic plotline of *Braveheart* demands. Yet Gibson's gloss on national character is patronizing and historically mischievous. His portrayal of Wallace is archly stereotypal. Wallace is presented as a sentimental leader, especially with respect to women, children and the lesser braveheart males that surround him. But he is also shown to possess vast reserves of steely resolve and fearless courage. Nowhere does a convincing view of Wallace's vision of Scotland emerge. In the film he never tackles the difficult question of what to do if the English are finally ejected. True, power struggles within the Scottish nobility are identified as undermining Wallace's position as leader, and the treachery of one faction that sides with the English is presented as destroying the Scottish cause. But the nature of these tensions and their implications for Scottish nationalism are not explored. Instead, Wallace's war against the English is portrayed as a family affair: the English were behind the death of his father and this death must be avenged.

To be sure, a good case can be made that *Braveheart* is not centrally about questions of nationalism, but rather is fixated upon more narrow questions of family. It portrays nationalism through the lens that we apply to our own families, as if family and nation are the same thing. More particularly, *Braveheart* is about the violation of family at the hands of others. Gibson has pursued this one-dimensional theme elsewhere in the *Mad Max* films and *Ransom*. In *Braveheart*, Wallace loses his father, his brother and his bride at the hands of the English. It is a big leap to move from the localized evisceration of family to the intellectual glorification of nationalism.

Yet the Manichean tensions in *Braveheart,* and the conflation between family matters and the nationalist cause, carry over into the other film in which Gibson starred in which British values are addressed at length, namely *The Patriot* (2000). South Carolina, 1776: the film's lead character is a widower, upstanding father and plantation farmer, Benjamin Martin, played by Gibson. Martin wants nothing more than to spend a peaceful, productive life with his family and the hamlet-folk of rosy-cheeked children, maidenly women, honest American yeomen and the clay-pipe-smoking, hail-fellow-well-met stereotypes that seem to exclusively make up this Hollywood version of the South Carolina settler community of the day. A veteran of the French and Indian wars, Martin was evidently bruised by the violence of these campaigns and is resolved to lead a life of non-aggression; he resists joining the continental army in the revolutionary war against the British. There are palpable overtones with the American veteran trauma over Vietnam in Robert Rodat's script, especially in the suggestion that all governments, be they colonial or American, eventually let the individual down.

As with *Braveheart*, at the crux of the film is the persecution of family and nation at the hands of the British. Initially, Martin refuses to participate in colonial agitation against the British. When his eldest son Gabriel (Heath Ledger) rushes to the revolutionary cause, his father is aghast. After Gabriel is wounded, Martin transforms his plantation into a hospital-cum-refuge for the revolutionary forces. At this point Rodat introduces the British nemesis, Colonel Tarvington (Jason Isaacs), into the plot. Tarvington is loosely, and almost wholly falsely, based upon Lt-Colonel Banastre Tarleton, who was arguably the greatest British hero in the

American War of Independence. Tarvington is portrayed as a monotonous sadist bent upon acquiring promotion from his bemused commander, General Cornwallis (Tom Wilkinson). For example, he elects to hang Gabriel, exterminate the wounded of the Continental army and burn Martin's plantation to the ground. Not unreasonably, Martin's younger son Thomas (Gregory Smith) attempts to intervene and is summarily shot dead for his troubles. This is the hinge of the entire movie. It provokes Gibson to resort to good old-fashioned *Lethal Weapon* mode. He launches a counter-strike, rescues Gabriel from the noose and hurls himself into extensive guerrilla warfare against the British. A series of ambushes follow, demonstrating Martin's righteous cunning and superlative marksmanship against the flat-footed foe. Eventually, American forces triumph in a grand-stand version of the Battle of Yorktown (1781), that leaves the defeated Cornwallis eager to take the first available troop ship back to England.

Rodat's script requires America to beat the British, but the subliminal theme is the victory of absolute good over absolute evil. The final engagement at Yorktown is portrayed as a sort of Miltonic baptismal ceremony for the new republic. It is presented as *Paradise True* because British stock can at last govern by their own lights, free from the remote Parliament in Westminster and its condescending functionaries in the American colonies. This resonates with American and other Western audiences, because it appeals to the same 'New World' logic that persuaded generations of migrants to come to America after 1776. Ideologically speaking, the cinematic plot necessity is to minimize historical contradictions in the attitudes and conduct of both British and colonial ranks, and instead to reinforce the revolutionary self-image of Americans as a race of the brave and free.

The tensions and divisions within the colonial ranks are certainly not seriously investigated in Rodat's narrative, although the historical case of the colonial spy, Benedict Arnold, is briefly dealt with. Nor is the heavy dependence of American forces upon military tactics supplied by the French, who wanted to extend their colonial influence in the region against

British interests. None of this is apparent in the film. Instead, Rodat dramatizes the conflict by using the central device of staging a somewhat implausible and clumsy battle to the death between the dastardly Colonel Tarvington and the God-fearing man of the people, Benjamin Martin, who eventually kills his opponent.

## Myth and Entertainment

*Braveheart* and *The Patriot* were not produced as history lessons, but as mainstream box office adventure movies. Their directors and stars were not concerned to educate the public, but to entertain them. Where is the harm in a cartoon version of history that at least tries to interest the public in the past?

In an age in which more and more people get their information and world-view from audio-visual sources, the answer is that there is a good deal of harm in misrepresenting history to comply with the plot-pacing requirements of a commercial adventure yarn. It is a dangerous substitute for real historical understanding because it reinforces harmful stereotypes and obstructs the development of a trustworthy perspective on nation and race. It reduces history to mythical clichés, of which the most egregious is the idea that race is destiny.

The military historian, Hugh Bicheno, for example, dismisses *The Patriot* on many levels. At the core of his criticism in his own book *Rebels and Redcoats* (2004) is the fact that the film is 'propaganda'. The skin-cringing arrogance of Tarvington with respect to occupied civilians has strong echoes of Nazi atrocities in the Second World War. Bicheno mentions an exact, disturbing parallel:

British troops burn a church full of non-combatants, an episode seemingly modelled on the massacre at Oradour-sur-Glane in

France by the ss in 1944. An identical outrage did take place during the war of independence, but it was committed on 7 March 1782 at the Moravian settlement of Gnadnhutten, by 'patriots' who clubbed to death ninety-three devout Christian and unarmed men, women and children of the Munsee and Delaware tribes, and took their scalps in order to claim bounty paid by the Pennsylvania legislature (p. xxviii).

This is not to suggest that the British conduct was without blemishes. Nor is it to imply that the Continental army were the only ones to commit atrocities. But it is to submit that the film deceptively recasts the historical record to give a grossly misleading view of British colonial policy during the conflict. Specifically, it inserts one major historical episode that is part of Nazi history and presents it as part of the narrative of British oppression. More generally, it contrives to equate the British with evil and the American colonists with good, so sundering crucial historical facts from the dramatic narrative.

*The Patriot* and *Braveheart* are symptoms of a form of popular entertainment in which facts in the history of Western violence are recoded and separated from one historical setting and grafted willy-nilly onto another for the purposes of drama and popular amusement. The result is an infantile version of historical truth in which the difficult and contradictory facts of national history are stripped down and relocated into the more emotionally accessible and contemporary world of family troubles. Thus, *The Patriot* falsely suggests that the supposed brutality of the British imperialists against the colonists is of the same stripe as the violence conducted against Benjamin Martin's fictional family and community. To put it differently, a national quarrel is transposed to the level of a dispute between a family and a 'foreign' bully. Contemporary audiences may have little time or interest in understanding the complex, ambivalent issues that produced the American Revolution. However, when a metaphorical enemy, in the form of a redcoat, points his musket at the son of an innocent farmer, they know whose side they are on.

More than this, it insinuates that the British imperial application of force is consonant with the indiscriminate violence used in modern times by al-Qaeda, and any real or imagined enemy of America. In this sense, the facts of violence are chopped from history and reconstituted as biblical evil which, in the eyes of American neo-liberals, is the mark, before God, of all enemies of America. To this extent, *The Patriot* cannot be regarded as harmless entertainment. It is more accurately read as one of the ways in which subjects are ideologically positioned by power to code the world in ways that reinforce national difference, inclusion and exclusion. They utilize and perpetuate myth to describe and distinguish national characteristics. It would be wrong to maintain that the Gibson films *determine* readings of British imperial history. But they do provide a predisposition, nudging or inclination for theming history and the world and positioning oneself in relation to it. This predisposition is neither arbitrary or capricious. It answers to a wider logic of assembling the nation as an object of identification for civilians who accept its rule of law, and distinguishing the nation from other nations. That is, it exerts an *ideological* effect over subjects *in* history by painting a calculated mythical picture of subjects *of* history.

Bicheno wants to expose the mischievous, calculated distortion in Rodat's screenplay. In particular, he wants to unseat the presumption that British colonial forces were uncomplicated instruments of extermination. For one thing, the British fought most of the war on the tacit assumption that they would be victorious. If anything, the British restrained the military advantage that they regularly enjoyed, by not systematically obliterating the forces of the colonists. A punitive, scorched earth policy would have bred generations of resentful colonists fuelled with a costly desire for revenge. Granted, British commanders were not always circumspect in obeying the rules of war; but they were not perpetually baying for American blood and mindlessly appropriating American soil for the Crown.

In response, it might be objected that Hollywood has always scrambled historical facts and national myths and mixed them with contemporary anxieties in the interests of drama and entertainment. Mel Gibson's portrayal of the hero in *Braveheart* and *The Patriot* draws on contemporary fears about terrorism, Iraq and the more obscure Arab 'threat'. Is this really so very different from films starring John Wayne produced at the time of the wars with the Axis powers, Korea and Vietnam? As such, to criticize Gibson for using well-established historical allegories originally developed in the days of the Ancient Greeks and Romans, might be judged to be precipitate and blinkered.

However, the salient point here is not these oft-used dramatic devices. Rather, it is the application of these devices to reinforce and perpetuate a stereotypal view of the British that associates them with racism, superiority and atrocity. The Mel Gibson view of British history as represented in *Braveheart* and *The Patriot* identifies Britain with racial domination, terror and a sort of inexhaustible, brittle *sang froid*. Viewed sequentially, they portray English medieval brutality and eighteenth-century British colonial rule as part of an unbroken trajectory of intolerance and repression.

The readiness of Western audiences, including the British, to accept this calculated distortion of history is interesting. It reeks of post-imperial guilt. The Gibson films play on post-imperial *angst*. They expose the brutality of Empire, without saying anything meaningful about the positive contribution of Empire to its colonies. Perhaps Gibson was influenced in forming a negative view of the British Empire by his history lessons as a boy in Australia. After all, it was the first British governor of the colony, Arthur Phillips, who famously declared the interior of the Australian continent to be *Terra Nullius* (literally 'land without owners'), thus eradicating the land rights and dismissing the culture of the Aboriginals at a stroke. Here British interests were identified as the only legitimate issues and British judgement was given unquestionable precedence over all others. It is one of the most one-sided and shameful acts of legislation in the whole history of the British Empire. Nor, sadly, does it stand alone. In *Imperial Reckoning* (2005), Caroline Elkins has recently reminded the world of the British slaughter of as many as 50,000 Kenyans in the *Mau Mau* Rebellion between 1952 and 1960. As with all colonial powers, the British were culpable in practising many acts of torture, genocide and theft on every continent that they inhabited.

Nonetheless, it is one thing to propose that the British application of Reason was faulty. The fault lay in the close identification of colonial forces with the assertion that the Enlightenment tradition represents the summit of human civilization. Politically speaking, this allowed the colonial forces a wide berth, for it wrongly conflated British political and military interests with Reason *per se*. However, it is quite another thing to maintain that the Enlightenment concept of Reason *inflexibly* supported colonial rule. Essential to the Enlightenment tradition is what Ernest Gellner later called *the ethic of cognition*. That is the right and the defence of an adjoining social, political space in Civil Society, in which Reason could legitimately be used to criticize authority and power.

To understand fully the Enlightenment tradition and its role in the government of the colonies, it is important to remember that it legitimated Reason as the source of *ultimate* authority. This applied not only to the application of Colonial authority but the right to stand Colonial Reason on its head through critique. This is what Thomas Paine did in his massively influential pamphlet, *Common Sense* (1776), written in the opening stages of the American War of Independence. Paine argued that the American Revolution was the first wave in a wider sea-change in humanity that he believed would eventually sweep away religion and despotism in favour of rule by Reason and humanism. *Common Sense* was a widely circulated, well-thumbed text among the revolutionary combatants. Later, the Republic honoured Paine for the role that his eloquence and forceful arguments played in the revolutionary struggle. The book also generated much debate among British and other European commentators on the question of whether it is desirable to manage human affairs around the rule of Reason or Tradition. Paine contributed to this discussion in his book *The Rights of Man* (1791–2), written as a riposte to Edmund Burke's dismissive view of the French Revolution.

Thus, Paine's arguments in *Common Sense* and *The Rights of Man* may be cited as an example of political and philosophical commentary in which the Colonial appropriation of the Enlightenment tradition of Reason was subverted and used against itself. Paine did not *abandon* the concept of Reason. On the contrary, he held that its Colonial application was defective. He sought to liberate the Enlightenment ideal of Reason from the halters imposed upon it by Colonial powers and restore to it the original Enlightenment associations of freedom, emancipation and justice for all. In respect of the history of counter-revolution in the British Empire, this is also what Parnell did to make the case for Irish independence in the late nineteenth century; Ghandi to secure Indian independence in 1948; what Jinah did in Pakistan, Nasser in Egypt and Smith in Rhodesia.

In trying to understand the relationship between Reason and colonialism then, one must acknowledge the fundamental importance of contradiction. The sun may have long set on the Empire built by Banastre Tarleton and his ilk. Yet for Gibson in *The Patriot*, there is no recognition of contradictions within colonial attitudes to the American cause of independence. Nor is there the wider acknowledgement that British colonial rule introduced lasting democratic institutions, the rule of law, mass education, public health, effective systems of transport and sanitation, accountable policing and many other civil, technological and scientific benefits into regions where hitherto, despotism, superstition and tribal or religious warfare prevailed. Instead, the Gibson films play to the arena of international half-truths, colonial prejudices, titbits of knowledge, juicy canards and unexplored convictions regarding British character. They mix up current popular international prejudice with old saws from the imperial heyday, which present the British as cock-of-the-hoop racists and zealots.

How far do the Gibson films compensate for gaps in public knowledge about the real history of William Wallace and the American War of Independence? Virtual histories of this type are fundamental in positioning global reactions to real history and the myths of nations. Of course, audiences appreciate that *Braveheart* and *The Patriot* are just examples of popular entertainment. But I wonder if the stereotypes and caricatures in these films are left behind in the movie theatre after the credits roll. We weave our perspective about the world and the roots of the present from many sources, coded and themed in complex ways. Films like *Braveheart* and *The Patriot* play a significant part in the process of ideological positioning through which subjects recognize themselves to be *members* of nations. They work through entertainment. As such, the instruction they impart is compelling in organizing popular perspectives of history and the present because it fuses them with pleasure. A pleasurable thing is a source of attraction in its own right; ordinarily we do not seek to find fault with the face that it presents to the world. Because we associate it with pleasure, we ignore and suppress intimations of ambivalence or contradiction. It is easy to believe in the myths utilized and perpetuated in the Gibson films about the nation because they are presented in such a winning, attractive way. But that does not make them true or helpful.

# CHAPTER EIGHT

# Celluloid Heroes and Villains

The Gibson films portray actual historical events in British history. They dramatize these events and distort history to equate British values narrowly with oppression and insensitivity. But Gibson is not alone in Hollywood in yoking negative values with the British. Ironically, the arch enemy of Britain in World War Two, Adolf Hitler, has been over-whelmingly represented in postwar cinema by *British* actors: Alec Guinness, Derek Jacobi, Anthony Hopkins, Frank Finlay, Alec McCowen, Robert Carlyle and Noah Taylor. British actors have portrayed Hitler in mainstream Hollywood films more than actors from any other nation have done. This is often justified as being a tribute to the classical training of British actors on the stage. But Germany, Scandinavia and France also have strong theatrical traditions. Arguably, the most faithful dramatization to date was Oscar Hirschbiegel's film *Untergang* ('Downfall', 2004) in which Hitler was played superbly by the Swiss-born, Berlin-trained actor, Bruno Ganz. Yet the relative absence of German and central European actors in portraying Hitler in Hollywood films is striking.

Surely, Hollywood's predilection for using British actors to play villains reflects wider Western cultural perceptions of the British as pathologically reserved and unfeeling. In the Gibson films, they are presented mainly as cold-blooded imperialists or – in the case of Tarvington – psychopaths. The British are imperious and menacing.

The associations carry over into other Hollywood blockbusters. In recent years British villains have figured in *Gone in Sixty Seconds* (Christopher Ecclestone); *M: I-2* (Dougray Scott); *X-Men* (Ian McKellen); *Last Action Hero* (Charles Dance); *American Psycho* (Christian Bale); *Beverly Hills Cop* (Stephen Berkoff); *Lethal Weapon 2* (Joss Ackland); *Matilda* (Pam Ferris); *The Silence of the Lambs* (Anthony Hopkins); *Die Hard With A Vengeance* (Jeremy Irons); *The Beach* (Tilda Swinton); *Conspiracy Theory* (Patrick Stewart); *National Treasure* (Sean Bean); *Rush Hour* (Tom Wilkinson); *The Shadow* (Timothy Dalton); *Firewall* (Paul Bettany); and *Inside Man* (Clive Owen).

## British Celluloid Villains

To celebrate 100 years of film in 2003, the American Film Institute (AFI) polled 1,500 actors, directors, screenwriters, critics and historians to vote for the 100 all time screen heroes and villains. The poll identified four characters in British history and literature in its top 50 villains: Alex DeLarge (*A Clockwork Orange*); Captain Bligh (*Mutiny on the Bounty*); Mrs Danvers (*Rebecca*); and Harry Lime (*The Third Man*). Eight British actors feature in the top 50: Anthony Hopkins (Hannibal Lecter in *The Silence of the Lambs*); Dave Prowse (Darth Vader in *The Empire Strikes Back*); Malcolm MacDowell (Alex DeLarge in *A Clockwork Orange*); Ralph Fiennes (Amon Goeth in *Schindler's List*); Angela Lansbury (Mrs John Iselin in *The Manchurian Candidate*); Laurence Olivier (Dr Szell in *Marathon Man*); Alan Rickman (Hans Gruber in *Die Hard*); and Charles Laughton (Captain Bligh in *Mutiny On The Bounty*).

Of the British characters, two are played by non-British actors: Harry Lime is played by Orson Welles and Mrs Danvers by the Australian actor Judith Anderson. Laurence Olivier, Ralph Fiennes and Alan Rickman play German characters. The AFI defines the category of villain as:

> Characters that movie-goers love to hate – and hate to love. Villains are characters whose wickedness of mind, selfishness of character and will to power are sometimes masked by beauty and nobility. Others rage unmasked. Daring the worst to gain the most, the movie villains we remember best can be horrifically evil, merely sleazy or grandiosely funny, but are usually complex, moving and tragic.

Are there any consistencies between the villainous features of the four British characters in the top 50, and the eight British actors voted by the AFU? Three traits are cogently expressed: superciliousness, emotional frigidity and near-psychotic levels of self-control. Lecter, Darth Vader, DeLarge, Goeth, Bligh, Mrs Iselin, Mrs Danvers and Dr Szell are united by a powerful conviction of innate superiority. As villains, they proceed on the basis that they are cleverer than and superior to their opponents. Even the working class thug Alex DeLarge, in Kubrick's *A Clockwork Orange,* listens to Beethoven while his witless 'droogs' are scarcely able to rise for a moment above the coarse animal drives of aggression and sex while their middle-class victims dull their wits and gorge themselves on a mixture of burgundy and *foie gras.* Britishness is equated with innate superiority.

Another characteristic common to these British villains is emotional frigidity. Captain Bligh rules the men on board his ship with a rod of iron, wholly indifferent to their reasonable demands for fair treatment and justice. The concentration camp commandant Amon Goeth shoots Jewish children and adult prisoners to while away the time as a substitute for hunting foxes or wild deer. Dr Szell drills into Dustin Hoffman's teeth with visible relish. Hans Gruber efficiently and coldly plots mass murder. The British actors playing these roles are called upon to convey the inflexibility of villainy. Mrs Danvers maintains a resolute devotion to Rebecca and a freezing indifference to the second Mrs De Winter. This is something that most melodramatic villains are required to convey, but it is evidently regarded by Hollywood as more effective when delivered in a British accent.

Extreme self control figures as a third characteristic of the villains portrayed in these films. Mrs Iselin is a double agent (again the identification with duplicity and British character), married to an alcoholic McCarthyite Senator, with a Korean War veteran son who becomes a brainwashed assassin programmed to murder the President. Laurence Harvey, the assassin, plays the role with the sort of vacant air of the worst sort of emotionally convoluted, former British public schoolboy. Hannibal Lecter, a cannibal and genius of exquisite refinement, is capable of playing a Bach sonata while frying slices of a human brain and feeding them to his victim.

Self-control suggests that you have something to hide. British culture equips its citizens with levels of reserve that foreigners see as unnatural. The constriction of the emotions in everyday life results in the creation of the British counter-ego. The hooligan or lager lout is Britain's modern Caliban. His lack of self-restraint embarrasses the British, and makes the nation an object of scorn abroad. Yet Caliban is so shocking because Prospero, a figure of discernment, self-control and emotional restraint, is so refined. If one adds the capacities to dream and imagine, the traits in Prospero's character are the standard stereotype through which the British understand themselves and are perceived by the world. By the same token, the British model of reserve is well suited for representations of villainy because it smacks of innate superiority.

Of course, the villainous traits that Hollywood associates with the British are not *exclusively* typical of the nation. Other non-British characters in the AFI's Top 50, such as Nurse Ratched (Louise Fletcher in *One Flew Over*

*The Cuckoo's Nest*, 1975), Mr Potter (Lionel Barrymore in *It's A Wonderful Life*, 1946), Gordon Gekko (Michael Douglas in *Wall Street*, 1987) and Kaiser Soza (Kevin Spacey in *The Usual Suspects*, 1995), have comparable characteristics. Indeed, it would be absurd to maintain that Hollywood regards the British as holding all the cards in the portrayal of villainy. All the same, it is striking that Hollywood repeatedly identifies the British, with their fancy accents, emotional reserve and public school demeanour as 'naturals' to play the part of the baddie.

## British Celluloid Heroes

The AFI defines the category of the 'hero':

> Sometimes mythical figures, sometimes ordinary people who prevail in extreme circumstances, heroes dramatize a sense of morality, courage and purpose often lacking in our everyday world. Heroes do what is good, just and right, and even though they may be ambiguous or flawed characters they often sacrifice themselves to show humanity at its best and most humane (www.filmsite.org/afi100 heroesvilla.html)

Three British characters feature in the top 50: James Bond (*Dr No*); T. E. Lawrence (*Lawrence of Arabia*); and Robin Hood (*The Adventures of Robin Hood*). Six British actors feature in the top 50: Sean Connery (James Bond, *Dr No*); Peter O'Toole (T. E. Lawrence, *Lawrence of Arabia*); Liam Neeson (Oskar Schindler, *Schindler's List*); Ben Kingsley (Mahatma Gandhi, *Gandhi*); Alec Guinness (Obi-Wan Kenobi, *Star Wars*); and Charlie Chaplin (The Tramp, *City Lights*).

Oddly, only two of these roles are about genuinely British heroes from national history and literature: James Bond and T. E. Lawrence. Moreover, the actors employed to play them have an ambivalent relationship to British national identity. Sean Connery, the most famous Bond, is a prominent Scottish nationalist. Yet his Bond is the archetypal British hero: an individualist, a fearless maverick and eternal patriot who risks his life for the nation's cause. O'Toole was born and raised in Leeds; however, he holds an Irish passport and although resident in London for most of his life he has used his Irish heritage colourfully to signal distance from the sober values of the British.

The remaining four British actors in Hollywood's top six may bring national qualities to their performances, but the parts that they play are not heroes purported to distil the essence of British national life. Neeson, a Northern Irishman, plays Oskar Schindler, an ethnic German born in Austro-Hungary, with a Londonderry air of calculated insouciance and *noblesse oblige*; Kingsley's Mahatma Gandhi is a scourge of the British in India; Alec Guinness's Obi-Wan Kenobi is a creation of science fiction; and the Tramp, portrayed by Lambeth-born Charlie Chaplin, is a representation of the romantic, urban everyman. These actors aren't portraying British characters. Nonetheless, their interpretation of the roles is recognized by audiences as bringing something recognizably heroic and British to the films.

What are these recognizable British heroic traits? Again, as with British involvement in the Hollywood villain, three traits stand out most prominently: courage, decency and modesty. Obi-Wan Kenobi, Kingsley's Gandhi and Chaplin's The Tramp have a never-say-die quality in their various responses to adversity. They see danger as an opportunity for resourcefulness. The Tramp faces a permanently bleak future, but even in his cups he has enormous resources of optimism. The British never give up. Neither do American heroes; but the British are much more matter-of-fact about their courage, less boastful and more phlegmatic. British courage is a birthright, and drawing attention to it makes the British uncomfortable. Even James Bond performs as a sort of auto-hero who would see it as bad form to comment on his heroics. Connery perfected this issue by developing an arch of the eyebrow to signify recognition of Bond's capabilities and disapproval of dwelling upon them in public. O'Toole's Lawrence would sooner die than boast. If there is an adjective to qualify the British relation to courage, it is rectitude. There is a solidity about this which is ideal for Hollywood's demand for undemonstrative heroes. This is why British actors are often the first choice for these roles.

The second trait is decency. Kingsley's Gandhi scrupulously follows the rule of law in using British legal values to demonstrate the hypocrisy and injustice of British rule in India. James Bond is not a rampaging killing machine *a la Rambo* – even his sexism is lathered with oodles of gallantry. Obi-Wan Kenobi is so far removed from brutality and tyranny that he seems at times to exist in a state of grace. British heroes try to be even-handed; they try to see and respect the other man's point of view even when they are committed to opposing it. This makes them seem more insipid than American heroes. American screen heroes tend to be naturally decisive and act from the heart, usually in the name of some sort of national imperative. British heroes take stock and establish a position that goes through the pros and cons before acting.

Modesty is the third trait associated with British heroes. This goes hand in hand with rectitude in respect of courage and altruistic decency. The Tramp helps others, even though he has nothing. Neeson's Schindler puts his own life at risk by helping Jews escape because he recognizes the injustice and immorality of the Nazi system; he treats Nazi bureaucracy with patient irony. O'Toole's Lawrence plays a dangerous game between the warped values of some of his British commanders and the strategies of resistance of the Arabs with whom he identifies. It is not a game waged for the greater glory of Lawrence, but for the common good consisting of both the Arab and British majority. The British do not make a song and dance of derring-do, they just get on with it.

That was certainly the case with the classic British postwar hero. Sean

Connery's James Bond epitomized British cool. He was refined and had good taste; he defended traditional British values, but was also *au fait* with the latest technology, fashion and cultural trends. Intelligence was the keynote feature of this image. It is evident even in anti-heroes, like the British criminals headed by Michael Caine in *The Italian Job* (1969) or the working-class secret service man Harry Palmer, also played by Caine in *The Ipcress File* (1965), *Funeral In Berlin* (1966) and *Billion Dollar Brain* (1967). They are simply cooler and smarter than their opponents and their American counterparts in espionage. In the 1960s and '70s, Michael Caine,

Sean Connery, the archetypal Bond, in *Goldfinger* (1964).

Sean Connery, Peter O'Toole and Richard Burton epitomised British heroic cool. It wasn't a matter of class, since Caine and Burton regularly played working-class characters. It was a matter of *savoir faire*. The British hero was presented as having a superior understanding of the nuts and bolts of everyday life, the angles that secured competitive advantage and the tangled web of human nature. This was a reflection of the principal literary, dramatic and artistic image that the British had painted of themselves during the high-water mark of Empire. At a time of expensive air travel, and what in restrospect seem very primitive mass communications systems, it was eminently sustainable.

To Hollywood, the British were a mysterious tribe. They spoke precise, refined English; they appeared to have a superior education and social connections; and they often affected polite disdain for the language and manners of their Atlantic cousins. A working-class sexist like *Alfie* (1966), in Michael Caine's brilliant screen performance, who expressed nauseating self regard and a well-oiled trapdoor mentality about human nature, especially the relations between the sexes, seemed positively exotic to American audiences. However, in the eyes of the world, after Freddie Laker succeeded in bringing the cost of trans-Atlantic air fares down, and satellite broadcasting made everyday British life more accessible to a global audience, the mystery and polish of being a Briton declined.

## The Rise of the Little Boy Lost in British Film

By the 1980s, an unmistakeable change occurs in the presentation of British heroes by Hollywood (and also the British film companies seeking a global audience). British heroes are no longer defined by *savoir faire*, but by their want of it. In the hugely successful movie *A Fish Called Wanda* (1988), John Cleese plays the barrister Archie Leach (inevitably an echo of British nostalgia here because this was the real name of Cary Grant, the actor who was arguably without peer in conveying the Anglo-American style of sophistication in the golden age of Hollywood). Cleese's character has money and authority but he is an impractical, emotionally constricted, ineffectual chump, who is seduced by the much cleverer and ruthless American jewel thief Wanda Gershwitz (Jamie Lee Curtis). Leach is repeatedly conned and humiliated by Gershwitz and her henchman Otto, played by Kevin Kline. In contrast, the British are defined in the film by their ineffectuality. Michael Palin plays the incompetent Ken Pile, the animal-loving British member of the jewel gang cursed with a strangulating speech impediment. Although Gershwitz eventually falls in love with Leach, it is clear that she is drawn to him by the desire to protect and nurture him rather than admiration for his courage, sophistication or animal attraction. What Hollywood now finds palatable in the British hero is a social misfit, a little boy lost, who requires the patronage and support of others to muddle along or prosper.

The popular global box office hits based in Britain during the last twenty years seem to show the British flapping around on their tiny, rain-swept island, hopelessly unable to get to grips with the world. British style features strongly in these films, but what makes things happen is American power and money. In effect, the British heroes in these films are reduced to mimicking the political role that Britain now plays with respect to America in the conduct of world affairs: Jeeves to their Wooster.

The perfect example of this is the commercially successful film output of Richard Curtis. *Four Weddings and a Funeral* (1994) and *Notting Hill* (1999) exploit the mannerisms of Hugh Grant to portray an upper-class, tongue-tied *ingénue*, easily embarrassed and perpetually aghast at the prospect of committing a *faux pas*. The Britain inhabited by Grant and his circle bears little resemblance to typical British life. It is a life lived by the moneyed, educated, leisure class, revolving around endless dinner parties, connections in the City, meetings with influential people and pottering around London. The regions don't exist in these films, except as chocolate

Hugh Grant in
*Four Weddings
and a Funeral*
(1994).

box destinations for a lovely wedding or a jaunt in the MG. Work is incidental to the lives of these characters. Nearly all the characters seem to live off invisible patronage. In *Notting Hill*, Grant bumbles along in a constant knotted state of just making ends meet by renting a spare room in his house to the charming but socially clueless Spike (played by Rhys Ifans). Significantly, in both films Grant's benefactor is an attractive American female. The lives of both the characters Grant plays in these films are transformed by the arrival of the US cavalry. But of course, in the age of post-feminism, the cavalry appears in the form of a rich, successful and can-do woman. In *Four Weddings and a Funeral*, Charles, his character, is rescued by Carrie (Andie MacDowell) and in *Notting Hill*, struggling West London bookseller William Thacker is improbably swept off his feet by the Hollywood movie star Anna Scott, played by Julia Roberts: Jeeves to their Wooster, indeed.

The successful Bridget Jones films, *Bridget Jones's Diary* (2001) and *Bridget Jones: The Edge of Reason* (2004), provide a telling parallel on the portrayal of modern British women. Bridget is a dumpy middle-class girl, played by the American actress Renée Zellweger. The ubiquitous Hugh Grant has a lead role in both films, but this time he plays Daniel Cleaver, a British cad, who seduces and then cheats on Bridget. Bridget is the put-upon, permanently beleaguered, ineffectual, chocaholic Brit, with a worrying dependence on alcohol and tobacco, who somehow makes ends meet and gets entangled in serial romances without quite knowing how or why. She is the parallel to the Charles and William Thacker male leads in the Curtis films. An important contrast is that she is not saved by an American, but an ersatz version of Mr Darcy from *Pride and Prejudice* – a legendary fantasy character in British female bourgeois literary life. Helen Fielding, who wrote the novel upon which the film is based, feely adapted scenes and characters from Austen's novel. She introduces Mark Darcy, played in the films by Colin Firth, as a sort of homage to classical fiction providing strength and purpose to Bridget's rather thwarted, arid romantic life.

### *Austin Powers* and the Real Meaning of 'Groovy Baby'

Arguably, the most globally popular, and therefore influential, cinematic cultural representations of Britons and British life in the last ten years is the trilogy of *Austin Powers* movies: *Austin Powers: International Man of Mystery*

(1997); *Austin Powers: The Spy Who Shagged Me* (1999); and *Austin Powers in Goldmember* (2002). Ironically, the British lead character in these films is played by the Canadian actor, Mike Myers, who also wrote the screenplays. Myers plays Powers as a camp, permanently concupiscent spy from the swinging London of the 1960s, who has just stepped out of an all-night happening at the Marquee or UFO club. His flamboyant, wildly inappropriate clothes and gratingly obsolescent catch-phrase, 'Groovy baby', establish him as an exotic relic of flower-power who gets by on sky-high,

Mike Myers as Austin Powers in *Austin Powers: The Spy Who Shagged Me* (1999).

deluded self-belief rather than talent, discernment and skill. 'Groovy baby' is a speech act that works precisely because its way of framing behaviour is so outdated that it becomes exotic, certainly compared with the equally all-purpose but much more lazy 'cool' that is now widely used to confer a positive valuation upon behaviour or situations.

The defining feature about Powers as a character is his redundancy. He looks, speaks and acts as if he belongs to another age. In engaging with the twenty-first century, he employs an obsolescent vocabulary and sense of style. His inability to cope with contemporary reality is registered by most of the on-screen characters with whom he mixes, eliciting patronizing affection and sympathy from the cinema audience. Powers is portrayed as inappropriately coded for the modern world. Arguably, that is how stereotypal views of the British are nurtured and exchanged in the eyes of the world.

Myers conceived Austin Powers as the antithesis of Ian Fleming's James Bond and Deighton's Harry Palmer. Where Bond outwits the gangsters and megalomaniacs that he comes up against by superior intellect, athleticism and guile, Powers makes do with happenstance, an awkward body posture that invites you to lend a helping hand, and sheer luck. Where Palmer has a rain-soaked, working-class chip on his shoulder and succeeds by class *reaction*, Powers is a sort of superannuated love child who divides the world into flower children and Blue Meanies, and yet somehow makes do.

What kind of Britain emerges from the Powers films? It is an eccentric, sentimental, passé culture that is out of keeping with the modern world and gets by on good fortune, endearing charm and tolerance to bad teeth and awful dress sense (intimations of the 2004 MORI poll abound in the *Austin Powers* films).

It would be wrong to maintain that the bourgeois picture of British life depicted in the Curtis films and *Bridget Jones* movies or the camp *mélange* of the *Austin Powers* trilogy is culturally exclusive. In the years since *Four Weddings and a Funeral* was released, other movies have shown

succeeded it, such as Gurinder Chada's *Bhaji on the Beach* (1993), *Bend it Like Beckham* (2002) and Damien O'Donnell's *East is East* (1999), involve much wider black  British involvement in acting, direction and production. These are far from being multi-ethnic movies made by genuinely multi-ethnic creative teams. However, they do reflect the opening up of multi-ethnic power in the British film industry; this, in turn, reflects the relative improvement in the balance of power between multi-ethnic groups in Britain and the 'native' white population. All the same, while *Bend it Like Beckham* is generally regarded as a global success, none of these films has achieved the international commercial impact of the Curtis films or the *Austin Powers* trilogy. Typically, their commercial career consists of a short run on the arthouse circuit and rapid transfer-

Shirley Ann Field and Saeed Jaffrey in a scene from Stephen Frears's film *My Beautiful Laundrette*, 1982.

ence to DVD format. If film helps define national characteristics, then Hugh Grant's performances of William Thacker and Charles and Mike Myers's Austin Powers have had more influence on global perceptions of modern Britain than Ewan MacGregor's Renton or Robert Carlyle's Begbie in *Trainspotting*, Ben Kingsley's Don Logan in *Sexy Beast* or Parminder Nagra's Jesminder 'Jess' in *Bend it Like Beckham.*

## The British On Film: The BFI Top Ten

Contrasting the votes of AFI members with those of the British Film Institute (BFI) provides some interesting insights. In 1999, the BFI polled 1,000 producers, directors, writers, actors, technicians, academics, exhibitors, distributors, executives and critics. The aim of the poll was to identify the top 100 'culturally British' feature films released in the cinema in the twentieth century. 25,700 votes were cast, covering 820 films.

The top hundred consisted of films released between 1935 and 1998. Interestingly, of the seven decades represented (1930s–90s), the most represented decade was the 1960s and the least represented was the 1930s. The actor with the most included films to his credit is Sir Alec Guinness, who appears in nine films, three of them in the top ten. Only one of the top ten, *Trainspotting* (1996), was made after 1973. Five were made in the 1940s, two in the 1960s and one in the 1970s. Hitchcock's *The 39 Steps* (1935) is the earliest film in the top 100. Only one film, Robert Harmer's *Kind Hearts and Coronets* (1949), was produced from the classic Ealing stable, which is widely regarded by critics as the high-water mark of postwar British cinema.

### British Film Institute Top Ten British Films of all Time

1   *The Third Man* (1949)
2   *Brief Encounter* (1945)

3   *Lawrence of Arabia* (1962)

4   *The 39 Steps* (1935)

5   *Great Expectations* (1946)

6   *Kind Hearts and Coronets* (1949)

7   *Kes* (1969)

8   *Don't Look Now* (1973)

9   *The Red Shoes* (1948)

10   *Trainspotting* (1996)

The top ten is mostly a list of dark films, exploring a range of troubling themes: duplicity (*The Third Man, Great Expectations, Kind Hearts and Coronets*); mania (*The Red Shoes, Trainspotting*); unconsummated love (*Brief Encounter, Great Expectations*); espionage (*The Third Man, The 39 Steps*); and murder (*The 39 Steps, Kind Hearts and Coronets, Don't Look Now*). Admittedly, the poll involved people with a high interest in and deep knowledge of the film industry. There is no comedy or light entertainment film in the top ten. The focus of most of the films is adventure and intrigue. Only one of the top ten, David Lean's *Lawrence of Arabia*, addresses the theme of Empire at length. It is far from an apology or celebration of Empire – T. E. Lawrence is presented as a tormented hero, split between in-bred loyalty to the Empire and sympathy for the colonized Arabs.

Leaving aside aesthetic and artistic considerations, this is mostly a list of films that concentrate upon variations of the theme of revenge. Harry Lime (*The Third Man*), Miss Havisham (*Great Expectations*), Begbie (*Trainspotting*), Louis Mazzini (*Kind Hearts and Coronets*), Sherif Ali and Auda abu Tayi (*Lawrence of Arabia*), even the stupendously ambitious ballerina Vicky Page in *The Red Shoes* – all want to get their own back against their oppressors and foes. These are, respectively: the British establishment, men, straight society, the complacent, insensitive d'Ascoyne family, haughty British imperialists and the tyrannical (and of course 'foreign') ballet teacher, Boris Lermontov. Perhaps there is a political subtext here: can it be coincidental that the main spurt of development in the British film industry in the interwar years occurred when the nation's position as a world power was gradually ebbing away? And when the second spurt occurred, in the 1960s, when according to the BFI poll the highest proportion of all-time British greats were produced, Britannia had obviously ceased to rule the waves and the final remnants of Empire were rapidly being dismantled. Was something connecting the main themes in films made by the British and the changing global political, economic and military position of Britain?

# CHAPTER NINE

# British *Ressentiment*

The French term *ressentiment* has been used variously in the social sciences to refer to repressed feeling, sullen, pent-up aggression, hand-wringing impotence, soapy nostalgia for a supposedly glorious past and needling, guarded resentment against a position regarded as inherently unjust. It is a condition of suppressed rage that perpetuates indiscriminate criticism without any positive aim. At the heart of *ressentiment* is the incandescent, scarcely coherent belief that the individual or group has not received its just desserts. The corollary of this is the conviction that other individuals and groups have been too amply rewarded, or assigned unmerited prestige. Another layer of *ressentiment* is that individuals and groups perpetuate the self-image of being the historical victims of myths of intention. From this bruised perspective, more powerful groups are always pulling the strings, coaxing the downtrodden and put-upon to place their trust in their hands, only to leave them in the lurch and betray them. The subtext of *ressentiment* is that oppressed groups always harbour the conviction that someone else is generally playing with their finer feelings.

*Ressentiment* is a complex social and psychological syndrome. It is most usually applied in relation to class – in Britain, the use of words, and the accent in which they are expressed, are powerful indications of social position. Nancy Mitford (1956) captured one aspect of its complexity famously with an essay on the 'ᴜ/Non-ᴜ' distinction, where 'ᴜ' stood for 'upper-class', which fastened upon the use of language between the classes. In Britain, the use of the word 'dinner' (a ᴜ term for the evening meal) for 'lunch' (a ᴜ term for the midday or early afternoon repast) is a *faux pas* that reveals a great deal about class, breeding, education, kinship and eligibility. Similarly, 'Pleased to meet you' as a greeting is associated with the lower classes, and frowned upon because it indicates an ingratiating attitude – for how can one possibly *know* that meeting a stranger will be a source of pleasure? (The preferred term of greeting is 'How do you do.')

In the British class structure, *ressentiment* is prevalent in the lower-middle and upper working classes. These groups are compressed between the powerful and the powerless. They occupy a social position that enables them to view – and sometimes taste – the crumbs of plenty at the high table of those in power. But they are unable to seize decisive advantage and are continuously fretful about slipping down the social and economic ladder into the hissing cauldron of lower class existence. There is a strategic issue of life politics here that is not so insistent among the powerful and powerless. The interests of the aristocracy and upper class lie in leaving the fundamentals of the social and economic system intact. It serves them well in consolidating and advancing their property interests. The working class has an interest in transforming the system and replacing it with a more equal, inclusive and just society. However, it is the fate of the lower middle and upper working classes to be wedged between plenty and privation. They mistrust patronage and reject partnership with the lower orders, without quite elaborating a tenable identity capable of leadership for themselves.

The ᴜ/Non-ᴜ distinction suggests that the nation can be neatly divided into two camps; yet it is no longer credible to assume, as Mitford did, that British life is coded and themed in polarized ways. Mitford's assumption owed more to the conventions of her aristocratic background than accurate sociological-anthropological evidence. This does not mean that the u/Non u distinction needs to be discarded. Rather, it implies that the distinction should be used flexibly, to apply to the many fronts of social positioning, embracing class, ethnicity, education and culture that occur in British life.

In the case of Britain, there are grounds for maintaining that connecting *ressentiment* to class is unduly restrictive. For a variety of reasons, there is a widespread and acute sense in national life that the British do not have their just desserts. At the heart of *ressentiment* are two splinters: anger and repression. These characteristics are not confined to the lower middle and upper working classes – as we shall see, some commentators argue that they are common, *national* characteristics, i.e. the British are held to be more angry and repressed than the citizens of any other modern, industrial democracy.

## The 'Basil Fawlty Tendency' in British Life

A casebook example of the anger and repression in the British character is the comedy character Basil Fawlty, from the classic 1970s BBC TV series *Fawlty Towers*. Conceived and portrayed by John Cleese, Fawlty displays a complex of insular, irascible attitudes and contemptible supercilious prejudices. He is sexist, racist, splenetic, prickly, pompous, inhibited with strangers and dismissive and rude to his staff and most of his clients. He has the lower-middle-class disdain for the idea of service, as if he assumes without question that service automatically implies social inferiority. Fawlty's chosen profession in the hospitality industry thus places him in a position of perpetual emotional turmoil. His suppressed anger is liable to surface at the slightest provocation or *faux pas*. As a small hotelier in Torquay, he exactly belongs to the uncomfortable lower-middle class, squeezed between the comfortable, professional moneyed middle class and the working class.

It would be an exaggeration to maintain that Fawlty embodies Britishness. As much as any other nation, the British have their fair share of generous, altruistic souls and relaxed, calm personalities. All the same, every British person recognizes the mixture of sarcasm, xenophobia, deference to higher classes, inhibition, and unease suppurating in Fawlty's character as familiar characteristics in national life.

For Fawlty, as for most British people, a meeting with strangers is not an occasion for candour or intimacy. On the contrary, it is regarded as more like a tournament of guarded hospitality and wary vigilance: the first hazard to be cleared in deciding if the stranger is of the right sort. Foreigners often complain that it can take years rather than hours or days before knowing if a British person sees them as a friend. The British feel uneasy with the 'buddy mentality' adopted by the Americans. In Britain, intimacy and trust are won through experience and time – in America they are presented as the opening gambits in social encounters.

Recently, via Australia, 'mateship' has emerged as a halfway house between traditional British reserve and New World candour and hospitality. The term 'mate' has involved and contested origins. Some experts hold that it emerged from the Victorian dockyards where it was hijacked and popularized from the position of mate on mercantile and navy shipping. Others stress the Australian connection, tracing the term to the mutual aid ideology found in Australia in the First World War. In Britain today, the term is a form of greeting connotating membership, inclusion and solidarity. It signifies a willingness to be involved in conditional comradeship. It is also a useful blocking device to be deployed when a difference in point of view or more serious disagreement arises. 'Come off it, mate!' is a let-out clause that registers disapproval without being insulting or provocative. Young Britons in particular, are likely to use the term 'mate' as an initial form of greeting with their peers. It is also deployed by them in handling distraught oldsters in moments of crisis or discomfort when the conventional British guard on the emotions is down. But it would be an error to interpret mateship culture as a sign that the American buddy mentality has made inroads into British soil or that traditional British reserve is melting. 'Mate' is a highly conditional term that carries the right to revert to the default mode of glacial privacy at any time.

In comparison with general New World standards, the British remain emotionally reserved in most public transactions. Yet, as with many aspects of British life, this should not necessarily be taken at face value. The Basil Fawlty tendency in British life may be read in an entirely different way, having to do with the tactic of using display as a basic life-strategy. This illustrates the dangers of taking the British on appearances only – after all, British life is the product of centuries of multi-layered social and cultural interaction. A tone of voice, a look in the eye or a momentary inflection can speak volumes, yet the appearance of things in Britain is by no means an infallible guide to their content.

Foreigners often interpret British reserve too swiftly as a sign of either emotional coldness or social ineptitude for effective participation in modern real-world relations. The error here is to confuse British *composure* with the appearance of bafflement, embarrassment and reserve. The tongue-tied, caveat-addicted British twit has an unerring capacity to get his or her own way. There are good reasons for this. Outward bafflement, embarrassment and reserve buy time to size up a situation and formulate a plan of action. They may also be read as pleas for assistance and empathy which place others at the beck and call of the person displaying anguish and distress. The infernal face-saving tangles in which Fawlty embroils himself are often help-cues for Polly and Manuel, his put-upon staff, to save the day. As such, far from indicating helplessness, bafflement, embarrassment and reserve may be interpreted as useful manipulative life-strategy displays designed to achieve tactical ends. The characters played by Hugh Grant in *Four Weddings and a Funeral* and *Notting Hill* and Cleese's Archie

Leach in *A Fish Called Wanda*, that we considered in the discussion of the British cinematic hero, reinforce the point: they all get the girl.

Anger and repression in British character varies with social factors such as class, gender, ethnicity and status. Yet they are recognizable traits of British character across the board. Too much can be made of the case that they are unique to Britain. In Europe, Northerners from Scandinavia, the Netherlands, Germany and Poland, tend to be more reserved than Mediterranean southerners from Italy, Greece, Spain or Portugal. Perhaps unfortunately, Britain's historical role in creating the Anglophone world of Empire diffused the notion that reserve, repression and the anger from which they spring, are unique British characteristics.

That the association holds firm today may be verified by considering briefly another classic character from recent British comedy in whom the Basil Fawlty tendency is palpable. Victor Meldrew, from the popular BBC comedy series *One Foot In The Grave*, is the grumpy, choleric, suburban successor to Fawlty. His character bears the same traits of suppressed rage, irritability, fear of self-revelation, awkwardness, pomposity and insularity. Like Fawlty, Meldrew is unable to achieve real intimacy and understanding with his wife. His antennae are permanently alert for any sign of solecism or slight, and he will tear a strip off anyone whom he regards as inferior or rude. Meldrew is an arch-individualist, permanently at war with political correctness and hypocrisy in a society of which he disapproves. Anger and repression define him, just at they pinpoint Fawlty.

Interestingly, as we shall see presently, the characteristics associated with Basil Fawlty are often considered as distinctively *English* rather than British. They look and sound right when delivered in the accent of the public-school, Cambridge-University-educated Cleese, when he plays the role of Fawlty with his nasty prejudices and ineffable snobbery. The implication is that it would be inconceivable for these values to be expressed plausibly in a character that represents any of the other three nations. Against this, Victor Meldrew is played by the Scottish actor Richard

Wilson, and Meldrew's dismissive, rebarbative opinions and exasperated moods are delivered in a redoubtable, bourgeois Glasgow accent.

What is it about life in Britain that makes the characteristics of anger and repression recognizably 'British'? The question has emerged insistently in the recent debate over the purported 'crisis' in British identity. Tepid about Europe, pining for the long-lost global authority that Empire vested in British opinion and undergoing pressure for devolution from Whitehall to national and regional assemblies, the British are in the midst of a troubling assessment of who they are and where they figure in relation to other nations. Two popular contributions to this debate have directly addressed the question of the place of anger and repression in British character. They provide an opportunity to try to define the place of these characteristics in the life of the nation.


## Anger

The *Sunday Times* journalist, critic and features writer A. A. Gill submits that anger is the key to understanding the modern nation. He portrays the elaborate mannerisms of the British class system, humour, the national love of animals and the countryside, political correctness and nostalgia as defence mechanisms designed to deflect and sublimate raw anger. His argument is a variation of the dominant nation thesis. Only in England, he maintains, is anger the 'default setting' of national life. However, because England has the largest population and the biggest economic and political influence, it sets the tempo of relations between all four nations.

In *The Angry Island* (2005), Gill contends that what makes England different is that it alone is truly an island in the cultural sense of the term. Geographically, all four nations that comprise the union are part of the British Isles. Of course, Gill knows this. His objective is not to stand geography on its head. Rather he is concerned with elaborating a metaphorical claim that only England is truly insular in terms of its national assumptions, qualities and values. Hence the difficulties that foreigners frequently have in deciphering English behaviour.

Of course, building an entire society around naked anger would make life with each other intolerable. In proposing a solution for how the English manage their supposed enlarged predisposition towards anger, Gill unwittingly uses a variant of Thomas Hobbes's classical political philosophy. Hobbes argued that the natural state of society is the war of all against all. His perspective does not locate anger as the primary mechanism behind this conflict; instead, he cites envy and the desire to accumulate wealth. For Hobbes, the rational solution to this state of affairs is a form of social contract. Thus, men and women agree to moderate their desire for acquisition and their envy and so allow society to prosper.

Gill follows a similar line of reasoning in explaining how the English regulate anger. In his view, they sublimate anger by developing a complex system of conventions, etiquette, manners, rules and protocols designed to keep damaging, violent emotions at bay. This accounts for the lack of ease, discomfort and embarrassment that commentators repeatedly submit set the English apart from other nations. Conversely, sublimation also accounts for the dynamism of the culture and the economy. For blocking anger and diverting repression require enormous creativity, ingenuity and self-discipline. In a word, Gill argues that English civilization is founded upon repression.

Gill is known for polemical writing that regularly uses vituperation to make a point more colourful or clinch an argument. In his book on Britain, this often leads him into some implausible and ill-considered flights of fancy. Take, for example, his explanation for the English passion for gardening. This widespread national pastime is popularly associated with good husbandry and English respect for aesthetics, and the garden allotment movement is traditionally regarded as a model of English self-reliance and practicality. Not for Gill. He submits that urban gardening is 'all repression and sublimation'. He regards it as 'displacement activity' allowing the English to sublimate blocked creativity, eroticism and distressing feelings of insecurity. He writes:

> More than anything else, gardens are the burial grounds of the lumpy, throttling puce anger of the English. The vegetative eugenics practised in mild-mannered cul-de- sacs, the extreme prejudice of poisoning some blameless green thing while feeding another, are symptoms of Pooterish yearning for a fascist order (p. 161).

Polemic uses caricature, stereotypes and exaggeration to clarify a state of affairs too opaque or densely interwoven to grasp. Yet Gill's use of polemic here does the opposite. It compounds opacity. The English may be guilty of many things, but a love of gardening is not unique to them, nor is the practice of weeding a symptom of a 'Pooterish yearning for a fascist order'. Gill takes the proposition that the English are singular in sublimating their anger too far. In doing so, he loses sight of the question of who the British think they are.

The Lowland and Highland Scots, both of whom on occasion label the whole of England as 'the South', have developed an elaborate system for displacing and sublimating envy, covetousness and violence. The French Canadians of Quebec maintain a distinctive sense of 'apartness' from the rest of Canada. This absorbs and reinforces a deep sense of regional disquiet that the language, racial characteristics and economy of Quebec is under threat of being engulfed by Anglo-Canada and the USA. Pierre Bourdieu's *Distinction* (1984), a study of how class and status distinction operates in France, reveals very similar mechanisms, forms of displacement and systems of sublimation. Arguably, this holds good for all Western-style, industrial democracies. For, as Sigmund Freud submitted in *Civilization and its Discontents* (1939), civilization is based on the renunciation of aggressive and sexual instincts. If this is the case, then all civilizations are founded upon repression. The English are no different in this respect.

In Gill's premise that the English have an enlarged predisposition towards anger in comparison with the other three nations that comprise the union, a flagrant contradiction in his logic weakens his entire case. As I have observed, his book offers a version of the 'dominant nation' thesis which is based in two stages of exposition. Firstly, the English are presented as the dominant nation in the Union, defining the cultural, economic and political framework in which all four nations operate. Secondly, English civilization is held to be founded on the repression of anger, a system of repression creating a stifling network of conventions and rules that are the source of both the emotional constriction and dynamic creativity in English life. There seems to be a missing link here. If the English have enjoyed centuries of domination, what can possibly account for their anger? It would be more plausible to argue that the key characteristic of the English is that they bless their good fortune rather than foam at the mouth, for they have been given much more than the other three nations that compose the union. Conspicuously, Gill fails to account for the *causes* of the supposed enlarged predisposition for anger in English character. This is not the only problem with his argument.

As I indicated at the beginning of the book, there are major difficulties with the 'dominant nation' thesis. It ignores the cultural, religious and economic differences within each of the four nations, and fails to acknowledge that Britain is a *configuration* of nations that are historically, culturally, economically and demographically interrelated. The history of one is so caught up in the past and present of the others that trying to disentangle them into four independent elements is an artificial exercise.

Yet Gill does have a point in maintaining that anger and the various devices to control it loom large in British culture. Only the Americans compare with the British in taking to indignation at the drop of a hat. The reason is the same. The American Empire carries with it the unearned

This reinforces her point that understatement is common in British life. Her description of British conversation codes is elaborated through a vivid discussion of the central place of humour in everyday life, the meaning of tone, understatement and disclosure, the social settings in which dis-inhibited behaviour is allowed (pubs, public transport) and the emerging new rules of transacting Britishness, through the use of mobile phones and the Internet.

As with Gill's less methodologically sophisticated account, what emerges most forcefully is the general significance of reserve, moderation, embarrassment, inhibition and wariness in British everyday life. In contrast with the USA, Mediterranean Europe, Latin America and much of the rest of the world, Britain appears to be a conspicuously uptight nation. Which, of course, confirms Fox's opening hypothesis about the deep and general character of social dis-ease in national life. Again, one should add the caveat that Fox's claim that the British are distinctive in these respects is less forceful when compared against conditions in Northern European nations. Nonetheless, her description of conversational codes in Britain rings true.

Her analysis moves from conversation codes to behaviour codes. The latter refer to the structure of personal conduct and interaction in social settings. The settings that Fox examines reflect the basic stages in which personal life in Britain is conducted: the home, work, transport, leisure, the dining table and bed. There is also an interesting discussion on the significance of fashion in grooming behaviour and social positioning. Again, the grammar of unwritten codes that emerges from this enquiry reveals the British to be unusually repressed, easily embarrassed, agonizingly uncertain about the meaning of social signals, obsessive about questions of taste and persecuted by uncertainty about the real meaning of social things. For other nations, social settings are simply the space in which means and ends are united to accomplish personal and collective goals. The British go along with this as well. However, for them social settings are also minefields of personal and social hazard. This anxiety about things going wrong seems to be acute in British life. Basil Fawlty and Victor Meldrew were conspicuous Jonahs, forever mistrusting others and expecting the worst. This anxiety may account for the general inhibition and repression in behaviour codes that Fox identifies.

According to Fox, British social dis-ease results in much of British culture being about compensating for the emotions that cannot be expressed in public life. She divides national compensatory characteristics into three parts: reflexes, outlooks and values. She also identifies the three core reflexes of the British as humour, moderation and hypocrisy. At all levels of society, these have been honed to spectacularly high levels of accomplishment. This is because so much time in everyday life is spent covering up or deflecting the symptoms of social dis-ease. Perhaps this is why the British tabloid press is without international peer in relishing embarrassing disclosure and sordid revelation. Everyday life is so manifestly based upon polite concealment and double standards that the fear of being found out is a national obsession. It is almost as if the British behave as if there is something awful that will be discovered about them by a little determined investigation. If this is the case, British moderation may be less about being cultivated and polite and more about wanting to appear balanced and reasonable, so that private awful truths are never publicly confronted. Fox makes the interesting point that the contestants in the British version of *Big Brother* are more inhibited and self-controlled than in other nations. The British often use foul language in the show but this, she argues, reflects the limited vocabulary of the contestants rather than powerful emotions (pp. 218–20). Sex occurs, but unlike the Dutch version, it is covert, and implied rather than broadcast live on coast-to-coast TV.

A reflex is a learned but automatic response. It is as if Fox is suggesting that, faced with being put on the spot about having to say who they really are or what they truly think, the default mode of most Britons is to ridicule, diminish or avoid the question. This prevents them from coming to terms with themselves or facing up to how they appear to the rest of the world. Denial is writ into national character, and the reflexes of humour, moderation and hypocrisy have evolved to prevent the nation from confronting what is being repressed.

The central characteristics of British outlook, Fox submits, are empiricism, 'eeyorishness' and class consciousness. The philosophical meaning of the term empiricism is a view which holds that all knowledge arises from the five senses. In Fox's hands, it is applied as a *portmanteaux* term in which the British tradition of scepticism against abstract, obscurantist thought is included with the national preference for evidence-based propositions. British 'common sense' favours the concrete and the factual. Accounts or explanations of everyday life that are perceived as too abstract or purely theoretical tend to be greeted with responses like 'you can't be serious' or 'do me a favour'. These are euphemisms for deep national scepticism towards arguments or theories that are seen as 'airy-fairy' or 'pie in the sky'.

Eeyore is the pessimistic, grumpy, blue-grey donkey invented by A. A. Milne in *Winnie-the-Pooh* (1926). Fox uses the term 'eeyorishness' to refer to the British tendency to complain. Grumbling about things, from the weather to the state of Heathrow Airport, is, Fox argues, a national pastime. It has a social use in that it facilitates interaction in a country where privacy rules. Britain is the sort of country where a grumble about the weather can be an ice-breaker in opening up a conversation between two strangers. It lends itself to caricature and exaggeration in British humour and irony. Eeyorishness is evident in the comedy characters of Basil Fawlty and Victor Meldrew. Their *ressentiment* is turned into a comedy of being peevish about things and constantly moaning. For them, nothing is ever good enough. A state of stability and order is just the prelude to collapse and disaster.

On the question of class, I have already made the point that Fox regards class consciousness to be fundamental in British life. It codes questions of taste, behaviour, judgements and social interactions. The British may formally believe in egalitarianism, but their system of positioning themselves and others in social situations assumes unequal access to economic resources, cultural capital and political influence. For Fox, although the primary salience of class in national life has been challenged by multiculturalism and globalization, it remains a more prominent feature of British life than in nearly all other members of the European Union, the Commonwealth and the USA.

The three values that Fox maintains define the British are fair play, courtesy and modesty. Her description of these values generally resorts to the self-effacing nature of the British and the phalanx of prohibitions against emotional expression. British self-deprecation is often false and uses understatement to conceal higher, more robust forms of national self-regard. Here, the discussion of the value of modesty shades her description of the reflexes of humour, moderation and hypocrisy complicates her insistence that values must be treated separately from reflexes. Her account of values repeats most of the observations made in respect of reflexes.

The exception is fair play. This is the foundation of all British sports, but, for Fox, it is also the guiding ethical principle of British interaction. Although the nation is rational in accepting that there will always be winners and losers, it adheres to the ideal that everyone deserves to be a given a fair chance. This is not quite the same as maintaining that every dog must be allowed to have his day. For the British recognize certain types of behaviour to be beyond the pale. The point is easily lost among European and American commentators who are struck by the bloodless character of British history. The Peasant's Revolt and the execution of Charles I are exceptions that prove the rule. By European standards, the British have been notably circumspect on questions of regime change and dismantling class hierarchy. While working class and ethnic mobility are demonstrable in British society, they have not swept aside the unwritten understandings, precedent and associated conventions that govern acceptable behaviour. The ideal of fair play appears to be applied to traditions that are in decline or disappearing as much as social, cultural and racial initiatives that are on the ascent. There is a 'live and let live' principle in national life that probably relates to the common law tradition and which has withstood the challenges of multi-ethnicity, class war and terrorism.

If Fox's discussion of the British sometimes reads like a guide to one-upmanship, rather than a reliable analysis of British character, it is an entertaining and valuable account for all that. Occasionally she lays it on a bit thick; in particular, her description of British repression is too ethno-centric. As we have seen, she regards inhibition, wariness, social curtailment and repression to be hallmarks of British character. But is it really tenable to claim that the British are notably more inhibited than the citizens of other Northern European nations? Scandinavians, French, Germans, Dutch, Belgians and Poles are also often regarded by foreigners as being somewhat formal, reserved and status-conscious in everyday life. As for hypocrisy, can a sustainable case be made that the British excel in this trait as against, for example, the Israelis with regard to their national policy against the Palestinians, the present fundamentalist leadership of Iran in respect of free speech, or the Americans with regard to their unin-vited presence in Afghanistan and Iraq? The moral is inescapable: so-called peculiarities of the British may not be so singular if they are subject to comparative and historical analysis of conditions in other nations.

Fox's central conceit is to invert the imperial tradition in which the British perpetually bring the supposed superior tools of British civilization to the natives, by turning these tools upon the British themselves. To begin with, like Gill, she seeks to narrow her sights upon the English rather than the British. Unlike Gill, she sets out to justify this by maintaining that England is a 'coherent', 'distinctive' national culture (as if the cultures of the other three nations are neither coherent or distinctive), whereas Britain is a 'purely political' construct. This version of the old dominant nation thesis does not pass muster. The 'coherence' of England breaks down as soon as one takes a train journey from London to Yorkshire. It's not just a question of accent; the regions have different ways of doing things and framing meanings. Regional differences matter. The cultural distinctions between Black Country people, Londoners, the Cornish, East Anglians and the people of western Lancashire – to name but a few – are significant. A Yorkshireman may regard someone from the 'soft south' as no more a part of the national tribe than an Ulsterman, an Aberdonian or a son of the Welsh valleys. Be that as it may, attributing coherence to England is as spurious as maintaining that Scotland, Wales and Northern Ireland are three separate integrated nations.

It is true that there are strong stereotypes of national character in all four nations. Fox notes (p. 22) that a good deal of discussion about nations revolves around them. It would be unwise to dismiss stereotypes out of hand, since they do not arise out of thin air, and to exist at all they probably contain some grain of truth about national characteristics. Conversely, to put too much store by them invites a rhetoric of nationalism rather than serious analysis. In the case of England, Scotland, Wales and Northern Ireland, stereotypes have evolved to resist acculturation to the English centre. This is one reason why the model of English nationalism is weaker than in the other three nations. As the most powerful partner, with the biggest population, the English have had less to struggle *against*. The three smaller nations have developed powerful stereotypes of the English as a basis for enhancing their own sense of difference and unity. Conversely, over time all four nations have borrowed from the cultures of each other, mixing characteristics through marriage, shared business arrangements, migration, political co-operation and the joint cause of Empire and foreign wars. In the face of all of this mixing and blending, it is difficult to say exactly what each nation has retained. In any case, for all of Fox's arguments that England constitutes a coherent, distinctive culture, in practice, her analysis (like that of Gill) slides into an account of the British.

Since her whole case is based upon the premise that there is something unique about the culture of the British, it is beholden upon her to suggest the causes of this distinction. She addresses this in her conclusion, which is, in fact, the weakest part of her book. She provides three hypotheses to explain British difference: climate, geography and Empire. The first two deserve no more than summary treatment.

The climate is an implausible explanation for British character. Fox herself makes the point (p. 412) that the British climate is not significantly different from that of other Northern European nations. Although much is made of the British nattering endlessly about the weather, they probably don't discuss it at any greater length than do the Northern French, the Dutch, the Belgians, the Scandinavians or the Northern Germans. In any case, why should four distinct seasons make the British more inhibited, uptight and circumspect than anyone else? If there is a correlation between rain and frost and introspection, would it not apply also to the Finns, Scandinavians and Lithuanians, all of whom endure rain and snow that surpasses the British climate in duration and intensity. If unusual changeability is attributed to the British climate, should it not make the national character mercurial rather than saturnine, open rather than closed? The climate has not made the British what they are.

What of geography? As I noted in discussing Gill's analysis, too much is made of British insularity. There are other island nations in the world. While the British may share some characteristics with them, they can hardly be said to be equivalent in character or temperament. Moreover, insularity is not a meaningful concept in the age of budget air travel, the Internet and mass communications. The old adage that what makes the British different is that they are an island race is further disproved by the national history of mercantile adventure, trade and imperial conquest. As island dwellers go, the British in modern times have more claim to spreading their outlooks and values around the globe than perhaps any other nation.

In fairness, Fox dismisses the thesis that the peculiarities of the British reflect the geographical position of the nation as an island race (p. 413).

However, she speculates that overcrowding has contributed to an exaggerated respect for privacy, eccentricity, inhibition, wariness and class consciousness. There may be something in this. In my visits to Japan I have noticed uncanny similarities to the sort of reserve, circumspect distance, brittle inhibition and double standards that one finds in British life, although coded culturally in very different ways. Fox draws the same parallel. But I wonder if this line of argument truly carries water in the age of globalization – Japan is as open to foreign influences as Britain.

The third explanation that Fox considers is the loss of Empire. She recognizes limitations in this thesis. The Romans, Austrians, Belgians, Portugese and others also lost empires, and they did not become like the British. This is a fair point – except one must add that the British Empire was really the last super-Empire in the world. For the mid-eighteenth century to the 1940s, its size, scale and duration dwarfed that of any rival European Empire.

## British *Ressentiment* and the Posthumous Existence of Empire

The spread of British systems of government, architecture, patterns of schooling, professional ideals and legal practice penetrated further throughout the world and left a deeper mark on global culture than any comparable modern Empire. This means that the British way of doing things, British prejudices and idiosyncrasy have a palpable global afterlife, decades after the end of Empire. Take a walk down Long Street in Cape Town, around Connaught Circus in New Delhi, down Queen Street in Toronto, Empress Place in Singapore or George Street in Sydney, and you will be struck by the British Georgian, Victorian and Edwardian designs of some of the buildings, statues commemorating British or Empire figures, the British-sounding names on street signs (Paddington, Kings Cross,

Surry Hills in Sydney) and the odd plaque or statue commemorating the history and place of these cities in the British Empire.

The loss of Empire is a plausible cause of British *ressentiment*. It was the deprivation of unprecedented economic power and global political authority. It was the sudden erasure of a role in the world that generations of Britons had assumed to be their birthright. Being British, holding British opinions and voicing British interests, meant less after 1945, although it took a long time for most Britons to wake up to the fact. It took them still longer to respect the voices of those who had experienced the sharp end of colonial history and to accept that colonization produced a variety of reactions to Britain and the Empire, not all of which were complimentary, that were of equivalent value to home-grown perspectives.

The sheer force of the motifs, systems of organization and architecture that Empire imprinted upon the world meant that British values, outlooks and forms of design continue to exert a powerful influence. Because of this, British global culture has enjoyed a sort of posthumous existence long after the death of Empire. Australian, South African, Canadian, New Zealander, Singaporean and Indian manners, forms of address, legal protocol, sense of humour and other ways of doing things are reminiscent of Britain

A British regiment moving though the very 'English' streets of Cape Town, 1900.

because they were introduced and defended by the British at the height of Empire. Just as Britain has a long history of adaptation and assimilation to new migrants and ideas, the colonies have made their own adaptations and assimilations of Empire traditions. Yet there are unmistakable echoes and similarities in the intrinsic national values and way of life of all countries whose history and culture were at one point forcefully shaped by the ideals and imperatives of the British Empire.

In short, the loss of Empire hypothesis as a cause of British *ressentiment* carries much weight. The traits of emotional repression, inhibition, humour and irony may have originated as eighteenth- and nineteenth-century defence mechanisms, at a time when Britain's global superiority was so ridiculously unassailable that bragging about it was frowned upon because it drew attention to a fact that many in the world found unpalatable. In the post-imperial context, these traits developed as strategies of nostalgia designed to hide the cataclysmic decline in Britain's international status.

The loss of Empire also provided the British with the unanticipated opportunity of rediscovering their own history. This has often proved to be especially challenging when seen through the eyes of formerly colonized peoples. For a long time, the ethic of national superiority that the British Empire proselytized, albeit often in a self-deprecating, manner, was an obstacle to hearing the voices of the multi-ethnic British who had different tales of Empire to tell. But that moment has passed. For much of the nineteenth and twentieth century, critical and radical thinkers pictured British history as the history of class struggle. While the salience of class is still recognized, now the turn is towards exploring this history in terms of the many cultural and ethnic inflections of Britishness. It is an outward-looking view of the dynamics of nationalism, rather than an insular model fixated on deeply rooted, enduring national struggle.

An interesting consequence of this is the emerging understanding of the limitations of traditional British solutions to British and global problems, whether they originate from the Left or the Right. The new century has found the British struggling to redefine their history in the light of multicultural and multi-ethnic perspectives and the national traditions of scrupulously repressing these perspectives in favour of the myth of a singular, all-encompassing Anglo-Celtic, Christian model of national identity. The British are learning that there are many ways of being British, but they have not yet discovered a viable language for representing unity through difference. The absence of this language is arguably the biggest bugbear against the creation of positive versions of British nationalism today; its potency owes much to the history of Empire, with its associated myths of British superiority and the charmed, mystically favoured life of the British.

The British history of religious dissent and nonconformity provided a cogent pre-configuration of these myths, which perhaps accounts for why the architects of Empire could take them over so readily and transpose them into a secular context. The vehemence of the belief in the absolute individuality, superiority and charm of the Empire is so totally irrational and disproven by history that it can only be of primitive religious origin. To be sure, before the history of the British Empire there was a history of the British Empire of religious *ideas* that is not often considered in the context of questions of Empire. John Wyclif's bible, which appeared in the fourteenth century, was a precursor of Protestant Reformation and emblazoned English style and individualism as thorny issues for Rome and Europe. In sixteenth-century religious literature, this was supplemented by John Foxe's *Book of Martyrs* (1563). This massive, gory recitation of the sufferings and martyrdoms of a huge range of victims – especially English protestants during the reign of Queen Mary – at the hands of Rome, embellished the idea of English exceptionalism in the minds of literate English and European readers. The historian, William Haller (1963) argued provocatively that the story of English suffering, religious persecution and fidelity to the true word of God, made the English think of themselves along with the Israelites as the chosen people. This apocalyptic, mystical view of English exceptionalism flourished in the sixteenth and seventeenth centuries and is evident in the political speeches of Oliver Cromwell, Milton's *Areopagitica* (1644), and the Methodist evangelical preaching and writing of John Wesley which imposed a hugely influential regime of self discipline and regimentation upon believers. Indeed, Blake's 'Jerusalem' also carries unmistakable allusions to the chosen status of the English nation.

However, for most contemporary British people, the Empire of religious ideas is not what they think of when they think of Empire. Rather, it is that geopolitical force lasting between the late sixteenth and mid-twentieth centuries. As we will see in the next chapter, it has produced a mixed legacy. Erstwhile pride is now counterbalanced by strong contrary sentiments of guilt and shame. On top of this, there is a gathering sense of anticlimax in respect of successive postwar political attempts to ditch myths of genealogy and design, which culminated in the weariness that soon set in with respect to Blair's 'Cool Britannia' project.

# CHAPTER TEN

# Empire and Phoenix

Without actually using the term *ressentiment*, George Orwell wrote eloquently on aspects of the condition in his essay 'England Your England' (1941). This meditation on British nationalism is interesting for several reasons. In the first place, it was written during the Nazi bombing raids on London. Orwell was addressing the question of nationalism at a moment when the existence of the nation was imperilled. At such moments, I have argued, national colours are nailed to the mast. 'England Your England' captured the phlegmatic character of the British, especially in times of crisis when 'there is a job to be done', but also suggested that the war against the Nazis was not only about vanquishing Hitler, but also about transcending a senescent Britain and replacing it with something new and extraordinary.

In the eyes of Orwell, the era of Empire was definitively at an end. He argued that the 'stagnation' of this system was apparent to most ordinary British people as early as the start of the 1930s. The war accelerated a process of inevitable imperial decline. The vicissitudes of the war effort raised deep-seated doubts about the quality of leadership in the country. The failure to stop Hitler's ascent in Germany and British defeats in Asia and Northern Europe created a popular mood of antagonism against the ruling class. Characteristically, Orwell was upbeat about political unrest at home. He regarded the end of Empire and the dissatisfaction with the ruling class as an opportunity for national liberation based upon socialist principles. The nation, he maintained, 'is a family with the wrong members in control'.

As we saw in chapter Two, there are powerful reasons for objecting to the metaphor of the family as a synonym of national life. However, Orwell is so compelling in following the metaphor through that it is worth examining his argument further. By 'the wrong members' he means not just, predictably, the rich. He includes 'the querulous press' already fulminating against the prospect of Britain's decline as a world power, and the dominant style of the British left-wing intelligentsia of the day, which he labels 'unpatriotic' and 'sniggering'. Orwell is manifestly in favour of the older socialist tradition which identifies the central objectives of reform and national government as divesting the ruling class of its privilege, the nationalization of vital industries, the provision of welfare and respect for national identity.

At the same time, he perceived that the end of Empire encouraged reactionary responses in politics, the media and the nation. In a wartime letter to the *Partisan Review* he referred dismissively to the rise of the 'blimpocracy' in response to the disintegration of Empire. It is this group in which *ressentiment* was concentrated, as they witnessed the elimination of their privileged access to the economic, political and cultural wealth of Empire. For them, duty had become decoupled from *raison d'etre*. The disappearance of Empire had left them without a clear sense of purpose. Because their sense of honour was so closely tied to the ideal of imperial duty, they were left with the bitter taste of rejection at the hands of both the socialist vanguard in the ascent in the UK and what they saw as the hubris of the independent peoples of the colonies. Yet Orwell considered their discontent to be manageable. He believed that nationalizing the assets of the capitalist class, whose stark self-interest had been partly responsible for propelling Britain into war, would lay the egg from which the British phoenix would hatch.

The end of the war momentarily justified Orwell's optimism. The 1945 Labour government capitalized on a mass yearning for a fresh start in Britain. Primary industries and the railway system were nationalized, and the state resolved to treat all of the people as the real national wealth of the country. The creation of the National Health Service and the expansion of state education were 'new Britain' to the life. However, the mood of exuberance was erratic and unsustainable. As India pressed for independence and other colonies followed suit, the national political and cultural climate in Britain became queasy about the economic future and the nation's slump as a world power.

At the same time, left-wing radicals were incensed that the crisis of war had failed to overthrow the capitalist system and replace it with full-blooded socialism. Already, unrealistic expectations about what democratic socialism in a war-ravaged economy could achieve were being kindled and exchanged. These were to prove costly for the postwar Labour government struggling to lay the foundations of the welfare state and invent a new post-imperial role for Britain. For the new socialist government operated in the austere context of national service, financial indebtedness to the US, the mass liquidation of foreign assets and food rationing. The British became burdened by a double bind of *ressentiment* accompanying the loss of Empire and a gradual, unfolding complex of anti-climax with respect to the emerging post-imperial, new Britain.


## The Double Bind in Contemporary Britain

It would be going too far to claim that *ressentiment* exclusively defined the mood of the nation in the postwar era. In the postwar years the British have been as cheerful, generous and optimistic as any other Western European nation. They have been protective of their families and have cherished their countryside. Yet the backdrop to national life has been defined by a culturally penetrating sense of loss and disappointment. The end of Empire deprived Britain of its traditional role as the watchman of the world. The welfare state heralded a fresh start. But the sheer immensity of the transformation in the traditional British way of life, and the necessity to make equality and justice the bedrock of the new system, created rolls of red tape that undermined the mood of national optimism.

The loss of Empire resulted in a long, painful, unresolved period of readjustment. Britain is the fourth biggest economy in the world, yet it no longer enjoys the economic supremacy that it took for granted at the height of Empire. The wealth that it has accumulated since the war does not compare with that of the USA, the extravagantly successful, profligate child that it created, but by whom it was defied and eventually rebuffed, in 1776. The British feel squeezed between the omnipotent, arrogant American state, with which it shares its language and has many customs and traditions in common, and the European Union, the principal countries of which have a long history of intrigue against the British and speak different tongues to boot.

At the same time, globalization, multiculturalism and multi-ethnicity have changed the pattern and appearance of erstwhile domestic institutions and ways of living. Building the welfare state required an influx of new labour from the Commonwealth. In 1945, the architects of new Britain may have looked forward to a future of roast beef on Sunday, warm beer, full employment for all and the chance for everyone to develop their talent. What actually happened was that architecture, cuisine, fashion, language and education were redefined through the complex adaptation between Anglo-Saxon/Celtic customs and traditions and the influx of multi-ethnic and multicultural influences. Many British citizens look at this and see the positive benefits of immigration in spreading cultural diversity, encouraging creativity and developing an atmosphere of mutual tolerance. Others see the regrettable decline of national customs and traditions and the slow death of the traditional British way of life.

## The Battle Over Empire

The British are polarized about the legacy of Empire. In *Empire: How Britain Made the Modern World* (2003) the Scottish historian Niall Ferguson portrays the British Empire as a civilizing contribution to world history. Without it, the structures of liberal capitalist, parliamentary systems would not have taken root and prospered throughout the world. It established English as the world's *lingua franca*. Ferguson estimates that 350 million people have English as their first language and 450 million speak it as their second language. Approximately one in seven of the world's population therefore speak English.

The Empire was not without faults. It often failed to live up to its ideal of individual liberty, especially in the early era when slavery, transportation and genocide were tolerated. Yet in the nineteenth century, Empire pioneered free trade. It created a global mass communications system. It introduced and enforced the rule of law over large areas of the globe. It brought effective systems of sanitation, health and education to countries in which these public benefits had been curtailed by despotism and dictatorship. Despite the fact that it waged many small wars, Ferguson credits the British Empire with administering a level of global peace that has been unmatched since its demise. In short, there is good reason for British nationalists to be proud of their history of Empire.

The diametrically opposite view associates guilt and recrimination with the Empire 'adventure'. For example, in *After Empire* (2004) Paul Gilroy argues that the British Empire was founded upon organized racism and maintains that its history was thoroughly 'bloodstained' and 'xenophobic' (p. 164). On this reading, the civilizing mission of Empire was fraudulent. In the context of the colonies, British doctrines of individualism, justice and fair play were masking devices that hid the 'systematic brutality' of 'ethnic absolutism' which tolerated the treatment of non-whites as inferior races.

For Gilroy, the native white British have yet to come to terms with the 'catastrophe' of Empire. According to this view, the British do not suffer from *ressentiment*. On the contrary, they are afflicted with a nostalgic, post-imperial melancholia for vanished imperial supremacy. In postwar British culture the permanent hankering for the wartime spirit of pluck and pulling together is really a type of wistful longing for an imaginary form of national homogeneity.

Gilroy argues that the keynote symbol of contemporary national unity in British culture is the remembered position of the nation in World War Two (p. 127). Before the entry of the Americans into the conflict, Britain was presented as 'standing alone' against Hitler. In Gilroy's view, for many native white British, World War Two was the last moment when the British were *really* British. Yet, historically speaking, Britain never stood alone against the Nazis. Crucially, it was supported by considerable and varied forces from the Empire and resistance movements in occupied Europe, and, of course, the USSR. Still, the myth of Britain as the sole defender of liberty, tolerance and justice against the Nazi jackboot is perhaps the last national myth of genealogy. It stands in the same line as the myths of Albion and Arthur.

British myths of genealogy ignore multi-ethnicity and multiculturalism: they are white myths. Gilroy regards the myth of wartime Britain as the solitary defender of the West as objectionable because it is non-inclusive, and smacks of the delusion of ethnic absolutism. It allows no room for difference and otherness. It exposes British hypocrisy in continuously dissolving the reality of Empire into misleading, vainglorious illusions that ennoble the imperial nation.

The achievement and validity of the British Empire then, is a deeply contested issue in British culture. Nearly 60 years after Indian independence, it is clear that Empire still casts a long shadow over British culture and identity. It signifies the enormous loss of British power and prestige, and also the carnal nature of British ambition and hypocrisy. One sees all of this in the pathetic existence of the British National Party (BNP). This marginal influence in British political life wallows in nostalgia for the days when the sun never set on the British Empire. Its current leader, Nick Griffin, believes immigrants should be sent home, capital punishment should be restored for premeditated murder, sex murder, terrorism and child murder and that the English language in British schools is being swamped by 'dozens' of alien, migrant tongues. These views are so abhorrent to the majority of the electorate that the BNP has no real political power. Yet its survival in 21st century Britain is evidence that support for the supremacist ideology that fuelled Empire is still present in the life of the nation.

## The Stillbirth of New Britain?

But it is only one side of the double bind in contemporary British life. The loss of Empire produced a conflicting set of traumas for the nation. This was partly a result of the swiftness of imperial decline. Before Indian independence in 1947, the British Empire was an immoveable force in the world order for over two centuries. Within 50 years, ending with the return of Hong Kong to China in 1997, the Empire was dismantled. But the anticlimax of the many bold attempts to invent 'new Britain' after 1945 has to be faced.

The various postwar solutions of state and market to Britain's post-imperial social, economic and cultural problems have had their fair share of successes and failures. However, there is a deep sense of unfulfilled promise about the post-imperial strategies to make Britain a country in which everyone is valued and has the opportunity to develop their respective talents.

The efforts to construct a new Britain around the welfare state are widely regarded to have unintentionally stifled enterprise by producing high levels of taxation and excessive state regulation. The association of the welfare state with inefficiency, waste and a sclerotic capacity to manage change, was part of the neo-liberal argument in the 1980s. The Thatcher/Major governments served notice that central aspects of the postwar welfare state were acknowledged to be so ineffectual and wasteful that they had to be replaced by the very market forms that socialism rejected in 1945.

Yet the neo-liberal alternative failed to oust welfare alternatives. The National Health Service and a commitment to state education are central to the British way of life. The welfare ideology of 1945 recognized the obligation of the state to care for the needy and create opportunities for the disadvantaged. Thatcher and Major both encouraged private health insurance, private schooling and private pension schemes. However, the best efforts of the New Right could not replace the welfare state with the law of the jungle in which only the fittest survive. Despite the electoral success of the Conservatives between 1979 and 1997, the authors of *The Rise of New Labour* point out that the electorate consistently recognized limitations and no-go areas in New Right attempts to liberate the British from aspects of the traditional way of postwar life with respect to issues of public health, state education and national pension entitlement.

Nowhere were the vulnerabilities of neo-liberalism exposed to more punishing effect than in the privatization of the rail network. In 1997, British Rail (the public transport provider created in 1948 by the nationalization of the 'big four' railway companies) was replaced by private regional companies. A private operating company called Railtrack was awarded the contract for track maintenance and network operations. The result was a confusing ticketing system with maddening regional inconsistencies in fare prices. Critics accused Railtrack of achieving no synergy with the rail companies. Fatal crashes at Southall (1997) and Ladbroke Grove (1999) led to a squall of media criticism alleging that railway privatization had been poorly considered and incompetently managed. The Hatfield rail crash (2000) resulted in the downfall of Railtrack and branded the privatization programme as a national scandal. The number of fatalities (four people) at Hatfield was relatively small. However, the diagnosis of the cause of the crash (tiny cracks in the railway track) created fears that the entire railway system had fallen into a state of disrepair and mismanagement. Railtrack was called to account for failing to monitor track maintenance. The company responded by launching a check on railway tracks throughout the operating system which resulted in mass cancellations and delays. £580 million worth of track repairs were implemented with disastrous consequences for Railtrack's trading position; the company never recovered and went into liquidation in 2002. If the New Right referred to long NHS hospital waiting lists and truancy and poor exam performance at school as evidence of the bankruptcy of the welfare state in the 1970s, New Labour seized upon the privatization of the rail network as the primary symbol of the folly of relying upon the market to solve issues of the common good.

New Labour presented itself as a modernizing party. It discarded some of the ideological baggage that had kept it out of power for nearly two decades. In particular, it rejected Old Labour's Clause IV, which committed the party to seek common ownership of the means of production, distribution and exchange. The politics of both the traditional Left and Right were regarded to be obsolescent in an age in which voters were judged to have ceased to be ideological. The 'Third Way' principles espoused and practised by New Labour sought to generate relevant policies to deal with the central dilemmas of globalization, the new individualism (the retreat of custom and precedent as arbiters of life choice), ecological risks, multiculturalism and multi-ethnicity. The Third Way relied on evidence-based research to identify problems requiring state intervention. The same mechanism was used to monitor the practice of regulation and provide transparency and accountability to the public. A positive business climate for corporations and individual enterprise was encouraged. New Labour's revitalization of the market principles introduced into the public sector during the Thatcher/Major years symbolized the break with Old Labour policies of centralized management and high taxation.

The concordat of 1945 promised a stable new Britain organized around the welfare state. Post-1945, the nation has been pulled from pillar to post in a series of seemingly never-ending doctrinal policy changes between Left and Right. One of the achievements of New Labour was to break this cycle. Not only did the Third Way borrow from both Left and Right, but it also identified change as part of the new global reality. New individualism was conceptualized as an adaptable, constructive, flexible response to accepting change as the primary context of social choice and action.

However, the problem with this acknowledgement is that it requires ceaseless policy innovation in order to create a sense of controlling change rather than becoming overwhelmed by it. In the third Blair administration there were clear signs that the electorate was growing exhausted with the inexhaustible programme of innovation. There are only so many times that you can apply a new coat of paint to things. New Labour's emphasis on 'monitoring' and 'standards' was unable to disguise a familiar discontent in British postwar life. This discontent centres on the popular sense that Labour's political aspirations have not been accomplished – namely, to build a society in which all citizens feel valued, possess equal opportunities to develop their talents, enjoy fulfilling lives and practice the responsibility of making and re-making communities distinguished by a common sense of identity, respect for diversity and encompassing narratives of belonging.

The British seem unusually prone to feeling short-changed by their politicians. This reflects many things. To begin with, the adversarial nature of the Parliamentary system lends itself to black-and-white judgements about the contribution and worth of social, economic and cultural policy. In the postwar period, 'new Britain' has been promised many times, but its progress has been regularly stillborn. 1945 did not create a society based on harmony and respect for the welfare state. Thatcher's election in 1979 did not set the British free. Blair's 1997 promises to build a new Britain based upon prosperity,

At Queen Elizabeth II's visit to Newham in London's East End during the Golden Jubilee, 2002.

transparency and responsible welfare provision collapsed with the debacle of Britain's entry into the Iraq War. The Butler Report (2004) and the Hutton Inquiry (2004) mired New Labour in damaging accusations of double standards and hypocrisy. The in-fighting between the Blair and Brown camps in the summer of 2006 exposed the central architects of New Labour to the charge that they were incapable of rising above the old politics of personal ambition. The achievements of the Blair years began to be re-examined from a new angle as old-fashioned, common-and-garden myths of intention.

## Trapped in the Double Bind: Muslim Britons Today

Nowhere is the argument that Britain fails to live up to its ideals more keenly felt than among multi-ethnic settler communities. Marginalized by their modest numbers in relation to the size of the indigenous population, the colour of their skin and their religious beliefs, they are caught up in the nation's unresolved sentiments about Empire and the repeated, manifest failures of the national project to build a 'land fit for heroes'. Culturally, politically, economically and socially, they are urged and pressurized in subtle ways to demonstrate identification with the native national culture, yet they are often the victims of incomprehension from the white British about their style of dress, cuisine, family systems and religious practices. As if to add insult to injury, their political beliefs and values are challenged by the British occupation in Afghanistan and Iraq.

Muslim Britons' incomprehension heightened with Blair's decision to ally with George W. Bush's decision to bomb and occupy Afghanistan and Iraq. For many British Muslims, this is an offensive and unjustified turn in British foreign policy. While Washington and London sought to legitimate it as liberating the Afghans from the Taliban and the Iraqi people from the dictatorship of Saddam Hussein, large numbers of British Muslims regarded it as the return of the Crusader mentality of the Middle Ages. According to this logic, the iron requirement of Western expansionism is to acquire an enemy. So it always leads to a bipolar world order in which 'them and us' models of belonging and identity are perpetuated. With the collapse of the Soviet Union, the oil-rich, anti-Western Muslim world has gradually assumed the mantle of public enemy number one in the eyes of America and the UK. This perception grew deeper and became set in stone after the 9/11 attack on the World Trade Center.

This terrorist act was seized upon by Bush and Blair to initiate a new and dangerous doctrine of righteous, illegal armed intervention into any nation that 'evidence-based research' deems to be a military threat to core Western interests. Hence, the Allies invaded Afghanistan because the al-Qaeda terrorist network was believed to be based there and Iraq was occupied after being wrongly assessed as having a serious bio-chemical capacity to launch attacks against Western Europe and North America.

The British invasion of Afghanistan and Iraq has inflamed many sections of British-Muslim opinion. It was the catalyst behind the London bombings of 7/7 in 2005, carried out by British Muslims and which claimed 52 victims, and the thwarted plot in August 2006, again involving British Muslims (23 to be precise), to smuggle liquid bombs onto trans-Atlantic flights from British airports and detonate them in mid-air. The incorporation of some British-born sections of the Muslim community into the nation has evidently hit some kind of reef. For these sections of the Muslim community, life in Britain is defined as perpetual *jihad* against a political system regarded as being stacked against them and a foreign policy that currently legitimates butchering their brothers and sisters in Afghanistan and Iraq. Culturally and socially, they are uncomfortable with permissive attitudes to alcohol and sex, and they disapprove of British materialism, tolerance of divorce and agnosticism. To understand this psychology we must remind ourselves of a few basic facts about the composition of the British-Muslim community.

According to the 2001 census, 46 per cent of Muslims living in the UK were British born. Of the rest, 39 per cent were born in Asia, 9 per cent in Africa and 3 per cent in Turkey. One in ten were from a white ethnic group. Muslims are the largest non-Christian religious group in the nation. Approximately 38 per cent live in London, where they constitute the third largest ethnic minority group, after Jews and Hindus. The next biggest concentrations of the British Muslim population are in the West Midlands and Yorkshire and the Humber. The average age of British Muslims is 28, thirteen years below the national average.

Muslim households are most likely to live in rented accommodation from a council or housing association. In 2001, 32 per cent lived in officially defined overcrowded accommodation. In 2004, Muslims had the highest male unemployment rate in the UK, at 13 per cent (three times the rate for Christian British males). The unemployment rate for Muslim women is 18 per cent (about four times the rate for Christian and Jewish women). In 2004, 37 per cent of Muslim men were employed in the traditionally lower-paid distribution, hotel and restaurant industries. Almost one in ten Muslim men was a taxi driver, cab driver or chauffer.

In 2004, one in three Muslims of working age had no qualifications, the largest of any group, although Muslims and Sikhs born in the UK are more likely than those born elsewhere to have a degree or equivalent educational qualification (Annual Population Survey 2004, ONS). In 2001, Muslims in the UK had the highest rates of reported ill health and disability. Almost 25 per cent of Muslim females were recorded as having a disability, as were one in five Muslim males (2001 Census).

What emerges from these statistics? British Muslim males preponderate in the under-30 age group. Most have been born in Britain. They are part of British society, but have no major stake in it. They are members of a community in which over three in ten live in overcrowded accommodation. A British Muslim is statistically three times more likely to be unemployed as a British male Christian; British Muslim women are four times more likely to be unemployed than their Christian/Jewish counterparts. Young Muslims tend to do well in the British university system, but their communities are deprived and the majority have no educational qualifications.

The Muslim religion emphasizes the responsibility of the community to care for those in need. It perpetuates strong ideals of brotherhood, modesty and mutual reciprocity. British Muslims have reason to feel that they are a disrespected enclave in British society. They were welcomed for their labour, but their religion and lifestyle are associated with backwardness and terrorism, and their domestic government openly participates in armed attacks against fellow Muslims in Afghanistan and Iraq.

Muslim faith is founded upon powerful principles of right and wrong. It is easy to see how these can be transposed to judge British foreign policy pejoratively and to dismiss social and economic policies designed to integrate Muslims into the life of the nation as half-hearted and insincere. Estrangement from British culture was behind the 2001 race riots in Burnley and Oldham involving young British-born men of South Asian descent.

More recently, two opinion polls of young Muslims born and educated in Britain, revealed disturbing levels of alienation. In a Channel 4 poll only half the British Muslims questioned thought of Britain as 'my country'. Shockingly, one in three British Muslims aged between eighteen and 24 said they would prefer to live under *sharia* law than under British law. Nearly one third of the young British Muslims agreed with the proposition that the 7/7 bombings of London were justified because of British support for the war on terror. An international Pew poll on Muslim attitudes reported that 81 per cent of British Muslims regarded themselves to be Muslim first, and British second. This is a higher proportion than in Egypt, Jordan or Turkey, and exceeded only by that in Pakistan (87 per cent). In contrast, only 46 per cent of French Muslims regarded themselves to be Muslim first and French second.

British red tape is doubtless no less maddening, formidable and demoralizing than French red tape. French Muslims probably stand in similar queues being asked similar questions by faceless bureaucrats. French Muslims are probably quite as disturbed as British Muslims by the prevalence of alcohol, under-age sex and single mothers in Western European youth culture. The French had an Empire too. This has left an unpleasant legacy of racism and ethnic absolutism in French culture. In a land that produced Jean Marie LePen, it is safe to assume that French Muslims probably suffer the same inane, offensive racial slurs and setbacks as do British Muslims. Yet their identification with France appears to be much stronger.

The reason for this is British involvement in the occupation of Afghanistan and Iraq, and French President Jacques Chirac's opposition to the war. For British Muslims, especially the first generation, Blair's decision to support the war on terror dramatized the question of allegiance. British Muslims represent 3 per cent of the national population (roughly the same number of people as the population of Northern Ireland). This is a lot of people to take for granted or ignore. British foreign policy made domestic undertakings to respect difference appear to be hypocritical. British-born

Muslims were forced into a state of introspection in which they reassessed questions of belonging and identity in relation to the traditional family and religious mores from which their parents had migrated and what appeared to be cynicism and insincerity in the land of their birth. It was a recipe for the emergence of extremism based in the conviction that Britain does not understand the beliefs and values of its Muslim population. It resurrected old negative imperial motifs of British superiority, indifference to diversity and doublethink.

In September 2006, Abu Izzadeen, the young British-Muslim leader of *Al Ghurabaa* (the Strangers) gave a controversial interview to the veteran BBC Radio 4 news presenter John Humphrys, on the BBC flagship radio current affairs programme, *Today*. Given the uncompromising tenor of some of Izzadeen's remarks in respect of the rule of law and government strategy in Iraq, it is worth noting that he was born Trevor Brooks, a black Briton of Jamaican descent, in Hackney, East London; he converted to Islam in adult life. Izzadeen presented British Muslims as endangered by the tyrannical Tony Blair and the legal and policing system that supported him. There was no room for compromise or moderation here, only a deeply entrenched cynicism about British tolerance and justice. Yet when Humphrys suggested that Izzadeen should go to a country in which his views might be more acceptable to mass opinion, Izzadeen responded with a patriotic statement of 'love' for the UK and suggested that 'deportation' for criticism in respect of national and foreign policy was in the minds of the British establishment.

What is this love for the UK that regards the law of the land as, in Izzadeen's words, 'completely oppressive'? In the first place, it is a mark of love for Allah who created the UK and 'the whole universe'. By implication, Allah can see through the hypocrisy of British foreign policy and is on the side of Muslims. In addition, it is love for the British Muslim community that Izzadeen sees as making its own way against the odds in a political environment that is systematically hostile to them. Another Britain is being justified and respected here, but it is quite contrary to the view of Britain espoused by Humphrys and most of his audience.

It is as if Humphrys and Izzadeen live in parallel universes of violently different assumptions about what it means to be British today. The tolerance, sense of fair play and moderation which Humphrys, through his references to respect for the law and the electoral process, implies are central to the British way of life, is dismissed by Abu Izzadeen as British cant and hypocrisy. Abu alludes directly to the use of violence to overcome British repression and he refuses to deplore 9/11 by using a quantitative argument, namely that more Muslims have been killed during the occupation in Iraq, than by al-Qaeda in the attacks on New York and Washington DC. It is an amoral argument that most Muslims would find incommensurate with the Koran, which takes a strong ethical stand on the Muslim responsibility to preserve life. Nonetheless, it is obviously passionate, heartfelt and delivered with a cogent sense of righteous indignation.

## Betrayal: Country or Friend?

Many of these issues have a long history in the life of the nation. The question of the balance in personal identity between national belonging and duty to kith and kin was raised in the 1930s, not by Muslim migrants or converts, but by the British bourgeois novelist E. M. Forster. In an essay entitled 'What I Believe' published in *The Nation* (1938), he wrote: 'If I had to choose between betraying my country and betraying my friend, I hope I should have the decency to betray my country.' Forster famously identified personal duty to family and friends as the hallmark of good character. From his point of view it was far more important than blind patriotism. It might be argued that British Muslims are following suit. Faced with the choice of siding with the land of their birth (which is engaged in violent occupations in Afghanistan and Iraq), or the religion and ethnic group of their families of origin (which is interpreted as the victim of the new crusader mentality), significant numbers have chosen to abandon their allegiance to the UK. As a cultural, ethnic and religious enclave in a nation which many of them believe is hostile to the Muslim way of life, they have acted just like nations who regard themselves to be imperilled. That is, they have intensified their sense of community and this has supported fundamentalists intent on exaggerating the difference between Islam and Britain. Winning the hearts and minds of British Muslim fundamentalists is going to be a challenging process. It is not easy to see how building inclusive narratives of national belonging can overcome the virulent sense of oppression and the attribution of supercilious indifference among the British political establishment to the rising count of the Muslim dead in Afghanistan and Iraq.

## English Icons

Part of the difficulty in engineering a new, viable post-imperial identity in Britain is nominating national icons or symbols that will be relevant to post-imperial, multicultural, multi-ethnic Britain. New narratives of belonging must be attached to symbols and icons that are plausibly inclusive. As we saw in chapter three, the attempt to create a national day to celebrate the nation posed more dilemmas than it solved.

We can shed more light on this crucial question by considering briefly the on-line 'Icons of England' project, launched and sponsored by the government in January 2006. This project asks the public to nominate icons that represent the nation. Nominations are subject to assessment by a panel of experts and are posted on the project's website (www.icons.org.uk). Recently, the alphabetical list of icons looked like this:

## Icons of England

| | |
|---|---|
| Alice in Wonderland | The Mini |
| The Angel of the North | The miniskirt |
| *The Archers* | *Monty Python* |
| Big Ben | Morris dancing |
| Blackpool Tower | The Notting Hill Carnival |
| The bobby | The oak tree |
| The bowler hat | *The Origin of Species* |
| Cricket | Oxbridge |
| The cup of tea | *The Oxford English Dictionary* |
| The *Domesday Book* | Parish churches |
| The Eden Project | The pint |
| The FA Cup | Queen's head stamp |
| Fish and chips | Punch and Judy |
| Fox hunting and the ban | Robin Hood |
| The Globe Theatre | The Routemaster bus |
| Hadrian's Wall | Rugby |
| *The Hay Wain* | Sherlock Holmes |
| Hedges | The Spitfire |
| HMS *Victory* | SS *Empire Windrush* |
| Holbein's *Henry VIII* | St George's Flag |
| 'Jerusalem' | Stonehenge |
| The *King James Bible* | The Sutton Hoo Helmet |
| The Lake District | The Tower of London |
| The *Lindisfarne Gospels* | The White Cliffs of Dover |
| Magna Carta | York Minster |

What is to be deduced from these findings? One might observe that the decision to focus on *English* rather than *British* icons illustrates the continuing difficulties in finding encompassing symbols of Britain. Focusing on national particularity rather than the unities between each of the four nations that make up the United Kingdom does little to help redefine a British national identity that is comfortable with multiculturalism and multi-ethnicity. Furthermore, the icons listed are overwhelmingly white British in origin. Realistically, *The Archers* (a long running BBC Radio show about farming folk in the English Midlands), the bowler hat, Hadrian's Wall, HMS *Victory*, Constable's *The Hay Wain* and morris dancing, are unlikely to be first and foremost in the affections or interests of the British Asian, African, Chinese and Afro-Caribbean population. Of the 53 icons currently listed on the website, only three have an obvious multi-ethnic resonance: in 1948 the ss Empire Windrush brought the first wave of migrant workers from Jamaica and Trinidad to the UK, and has become a symbol of the rise of multi-ethnic Britain; Brick Lane in East London is the focal point of a thriving Bangladeshi and Bengali community renowned for its Asian food and fashion; and the Notting Hill Carnival, established in 1964, is a festival celebrating the Afro-Caribbean (and increasingly, Latin American) population.

Like all nations, the British look for symbols of belonging in three things: land (hedges, the Lake District, the oak tree, the White Cliffs of Dover); history (the *Domesday Book*, Hadrian's Wall, HMS *Victory*, Magna Carta; the Spitfire; Stonehenge; York Minster); and culture (*Alice in Wonderland*, the Angel of the North, *The Archers*, cricket, the Globe Theatre, 'Jerusalem', *Monty Python*, morris dancing, parish churches, the pint, rugby). Of the current list of icons, only Sherlock Holmes might strictly be described as a myth, since this fictional character has stepped out of the pages of literature to become a sort of idol for a particular version of cool British intelligence, resourcefulness and fortitude. Yet, indirectly, almost all of the icons have mythical associations with powerful motifs of national unity, glorious history and common sensibility.

In his *Albion* (2002), Peter Ackroyd captures the myth of genealogy involved here with his phrase 'the English Imagination' (p. 448). By this he means a sensibility that takes the form of an 'endless enchanted circle, or shining ring', with no beginning or end and which moves backwards and forwards. Like Albion and Arthur, the English imagination precedes politics and recorded history. It is evident in timeless national cultural motifs such as 'love of the marvellous' and 'the delight in small things'. In his fiction, Ackroyd has walked in the footsteps of Oscar Wilde, Chatterton, Milton, the sixteenth century alchemist and astrologer, John Dee, Charles and Mary Lamb, and Dan Leno. In his biographical works he has imagined himself strolling around Victorian London and talking to Charles Dickens, and in his life of William Blake he has constructed a brilliant portrait of London between the 1750s and 1820s. Ackroyd obviously believes in the mystical line in national culture that has left its mark on the geographical landscape and binds English literature and poetry together like a marigold chain. Yet if Kate Fox in *The English* (2004) is right to identify empiricism, pragmatism and practicality as strong traits of national character, surely many English people will regard Ackroyd's reference to 'eternal lines', mystical, reversible connections that link past, present and future and the patter of timeless footsteps in British culture as pure hokum.

What it elides is politics and history – the primary influences that have made the British what they are. Dealing with politics and history so that no British cultural or ethnic group is excluded is the main challenge in finding plausible icons and symbols to represent and theme the nation today. We must not assume that icons and symbols from the feudal, mercantile or imperial past will work in post-imperial, multicultural and multi-ethnic Britain. This is because a good number of these symbols – Hadrian's Wall, HMS *Victory*, the *King James Bible*, the *Lindisfarne Gospels*, parish churches and the ss *Empire Windrush* – are enmeshed with complex facts and mythologies of British supremacy, British exceptionalism and the British right to a violence over bodies, spaces and ideas. The task is to find ways of recognizing the contribution of voices belittled and stifled by the intransigent, unwritten right of priority and outright domination given to the mother country.

Attempting to recode traditional British icons and symbols of nationhood overnight in order to embrace multicultural and multi-ethnic particularities is unlikely to succeed, since there is a lot of problematic history to undo. This book has proposed that nations have the strongest sense of themselves *as nations* when they are imperilled. In Britain the key moments in this respect occurred when the nation regarded itself as white, Christian and implacably affixed to Anglo-Saxon/Celtic values. Yet for Britons today, the imagery which appeals to national virtue in the face of Nazi fascism seems as remote and meaningless as Agincourt. The nation of 1940 is scarcely recognizable today. Any attempt to create new symbols of contemporary nationality has to recognize that privilege can no longer be assigned to the white, Christian Anglo-Saxon/Celtic way of life. There are many Britains now and we need to recognize that a new dynamics and politics of nationalism are required in order to embrace them.

Benedict Anderson's *Imagined Communities* (1983) taught us that nations are 'imagined communities'. Part of the challenge facing modern Britain is to imagine ourselves freed from a history based on organized class inequality and racial oppression, and instead to embrace the multi-ethnic, multicultural, global realities of the world in which we now live. An *esprit d'corps* will not be achieved by appealing to Churchill, Dunkirk or VE day. This is because some of the people called upon to celebrate these historical icons in British history regard themselves and their ancestors to be victims of British hubris and insensitivity.

## The Parekh Report

The task of finding new symbols of national belonging and unity that will be relevant to multicultural, multi-ethnic Britain will be a long and arduous one. In 2000, the Parekh Report on the future of multi-ethnic Britain, commissioned by The Runnymede Trust, made a number of well-considered recommendations based around recognizing cohesion, difference and equality as cardinal values for British citizens today. It insisted that these values must inform and shape the reforming of policing, reducing racial inequalities, expanding access and participation in sport, culture, the media and education and increasing black, Asian and Irish representation in health and welfare. The Report called for an Equality Act to enshrine these values and organizational requirements in a single piece of legislation. By extension, it recommended the establishment of an Equality Commission to enforce and monitor these anti-racist values of cohesion, difference and equality.

The Report noted that postwar migration and the emergence of first and second generations of black Britons and Asian Britons, globalization and multiculturalism have coalesced to change traditional notions of national identity. In order to combat 'multi-ethnic drift', it advocated defining a new positive vision of Britain as 'the community of communities' which recognizes value in all citizens and provided equal opportunities for all to lead fulfilling lives. Parekh regarded the achievement of this objective as involving six interconnecting themes:

1 Rethinking the national story and national identity.
2 Understanding that all identities are in a process of transition.
3 Developing a balance between cohesion, equality and difference.
4 Addressing and eliminating all forms of racism.
5 Reducing material inequalities.
6 Building a pluralistic human rights culture.

In general, the recommendations were well received. However, the tabloid press rounded on the section in the Report on 'rethinking the national story and national identity'. This theme sought to address the question of social inclusion in contemporary Britain by bringing in the voices that had been marginalized by traditional versions of British history.

In the 1960s, historians such as E. P. Thompson and Christopher Hill challenged the orthodoxy among British historians by demanding the need to rethink the national story from the perspective of the working class. Implicit in the Parekh Report is the judgement that something similar is warranted today, in respect of the perspectives and contributions of multi-ethnic communities in British history and marginalized multicultural groups that were 'written out' of the official version of the national story. Having rediscovered the working class in the making of English history, it is time to be more rigorously inclusive and rediscover the part played by multi-ethnic and multicultural groups.

The tabloid press tore into this section of the report as a move by faceless bureaucrats and do-gooders to rob the British of their history and replace it with a bland alternative constructed by committee. According to the tabloids, what made Britain 'great' is the long history of bloody-minded exceptionalism, inventiveness and courage in the face of adversity. Replacing this with Parekh's vision of Britain as 'the community of communities' was condemned as both glib and sterile.

There is a difficult point to address here. The ideology of Empire legitimated the use of physical violence in order to enhance justice, liberty and democracy. The advance of these central values in Western civilization was coupled with progress. Historically, the battles and wars fought in the name of Empire were justified as contributions to this cause. Avarice, gluttony and lust were part and parcel of this enterprise. Yet it would be a mistake to ignore the fact that to many people in the nation it was ideologically justified as an elevated, noble cause, an end worth fighting and dying for.

We see Empire differently these days. To regard British violence over colonized bodies and occupied space as a necessary part of pursuing the higher goal of progress now smacks of bigotry. We have too much knowledge of the many-sided character of Empire, so reconciliation to the ideal of Empire as a completely noble project is problematic. Any positive identification that the British feel with the imperial order as the summit of national achievement is now tinged with estrangement from the unempathetic, slash-and-burn tactics that followed the imperial handcart.

I proposed earlier that the British have deeply polarized views about Empire. As such, it is perhaps best to neither endorse or reject it, but to seek a more prosaic way of reading it as a *double-coded* enterprise. It did advance justice, liberty and democracy, but it also failed regularly to live up to these ideals, favouring British interests over ecumenical strategies of including the colonized peoples. In effect, this is what the Parekh Report enjoins.

The challenge of reading Empire as doubly-coded is to overcome the folklore myths that have surrounded the history of Empire. It is one thing to posit cohesion, equality and difference as hinges for building new narratives of belonging in a Britain which acknowledges multiculturalism and multi-ethnicity. But the task is up against a colourful, emotive imperial history that includes Robert Clive's defeat of the Nawab of Bengal at the Battle of Plassey (1757), which gave the British ascendancy in India; the defeat of the French and the death of the British commander General Wolfe on the Plains of Abraham (1759), which secured Canada for the British; the battle of Rorke's Drift in South Africa (1879) – the subject of the hugely successful adventure movie *Zulu* (1964) – in which a small British expeditionary force withstood a mass Zulu assault, for which action they won the highest number of Victoria Crosses (eleven) ever awarded for a single engagement; and the Battle of Omdurman (1898) in Egypt, where British-Egyptian-Sudanese troops led by Lord Kitchener defeated the Mahdist army – symbolic revenge for the death of General Gordon in Khartoum in 1885.

The most sensible conclusion is to accept that plausible symbols of belonging and unity to which all Britons, regardless of class, creed and colour can be emotionally attached, will not be built overnight. History will supply these symbols. Sadly, the main catalysts here will be toil and trouble, because it is when the nation is most under threat that solidarity and unity are most keenly expressed. But the achievement of ends through common endeavour, creating successes for the nation through co-operation in business, industry, sport and the arts, is also a way of building unity through difference. It is vital that policies of social and economic inclusion are applied and supported. Otherwise the future on all sides is one of chronic, cancerous British *ressentiment*.

CHAPTER ELEVEN

# The Citizenship Test

A direct result of the Parekh Report was the introduction of 'citizenship ceremonies', for all who are accepted for evaluation by the Home Office to become eligible for British naturalization. Parekh lamented the naturalization process of the day. It was dismissed for being antiseptic, inhospitable and over-bureaucratic. As an alternative, Parekh called for a ceremony that would enable new citizens to receive a less reserved welcome from their fellow citizens. The ceremonies were intended to be a celebration of being, and becoming, British.

Under the terms of the Nationality, Immigration and Asylum Act (2002), naturalization and registration involve taking a citizenship oath and making a pledge at a citizenship ceremony. Prospective citizens are required to make an oath or affirmation to the Queen and a pledge of loyalty to the United Kingdom. Typically, ceremonies begin with a welcoming address by the Superintendent Registrar. They include uplifting speeches by local dignitaries on what being British means. New citizens receive a certificate of nationality, an information pack and commemorative gifts. The ceremonies end with playing the national anthem.

*you have to learn About Britain*
*if you want to live here*

On average 140,000 prospective citizens apply for British nationality every year. In order to be eligible, applicants must have resided in the country for five years and possess a working knowledge of English. On average, 20 per cent of applicants do not meet the necessary standard on language; they are required to study English and achieve the level of competence before reapplying.

In 2005, the naturalization process was extended to include the so-called 'citizenship test'. Candidates were required to answer 24 multiple-choice questions designed to assess their knowledge of life in Britain. The questions presuppose that candidates have read the 'Life In Britain' document produced by the Home Office, which aims to provide a guide to the British way of life and underlying national values. Sample questions include:

Select the correct answer.

*Which of these courts uses a jury system?*
Magistrates' court
Crown court
Youth court
County court

*Is the statement below TRUE or FALSE?*
Your employer can dismiss you for joining a trade union.

*Which TWO telephone numbers can be used to dial the emergency services?*
112 123 555 999

*Which of these statements is correct?*
A television licence is required for each television in a home.
A single television licence covers all televisions in a home.

*The changing role of women*

Do women have equal rights and has this always been the case?

Are there as many women in education or work as men?

Do women have the same pay as men?

Do women with children work?

*Children, family and young people*

How many young people are there in the UK?

Do many children live in single-parent families or step-families?

When do children leave home?

What sort of work do children do?

When do children take tests at school? How many go on to
higher education?

What are the minimum ages for buying alcohol and tobacco?

What drugs are illegal?

How interested are young people in politics? What do they see as
the main issues today?

*The regions of Britain*

Where are the Geordie, cockney and scouse dialects spoken?

*Customs and traditions*

Do people tend to live in cities or in the country?

What and when are the national days of the four countries of the
UK? What are bank holidays?

What and when are the main Christian festivals? What other
traditional days are celebrated?

*The working system of government*

What are MPs? How often are elections held and who forms the
government?

What is the role of the Prime Minister? Who advises them and
what are the main roles in cabinet?

What type of constitution does the UK have? What is Her
Majesty's Opposition and what is the role of the Leader of the
Opposition?

How is political debate reported? Are newspapers free to publish
opinions or do they have to remain impartial?

*The formal institutions (1)*

What is the Queen's official role and what ceremonial duties
does she have?

How do elections for the House of Commons work? How are
candidates selected? What do the speaker and whips do?
What is the House of Lords and who are its members?
How can you visit Parliament?

*The formal institutions (2)*

How are judges appointed and how do they apply the law?

How are the police organized and who controls their
adminstration?

What is the civil service and how do civil servants work with
government?

How are local services managed, governed and paid for?

The test focuses primarily on the practical, day-to-day knowledge with
which citizens need to be conversant in order to define themselves and be
defined by others as British. The emphasis on practical knowledge and
mastery of the language provide testament to the continuing strength of
pragmatism as a trait of the British way. As noted, oaths of allegiance to
the Queen and the United Kingdom are required. But they are expressed
at such a high level of generality that they are more properly described as

gestures rather than contractual duties and responsibilities.

The Home Office primer that accompanies the citizenship test, 'Life in the United Kingdom', is anodyne. It submits that the British offer equal opportunity for everyone to fulfil their talents irrespective of class, colour or creed. In return, they expect and demand responsibility and an acceptance of common standards, rules of behaviour and mutual tolerance. Many of the aspiring citizens will have come from disadvantaged sections of the community where the claim to offer equal opportunity is routinely regarded as an example of British humbug. As a result, the acceptance of common standards and rules is probably practised strategically and tactically as a matter of life politics.

Instead of accepting the responsibility for discovering why common standards and rules are regarded as oppressive national *enforcement* by some sections of the community, or really determining what it means to

The Houses of Parliament, London.

give everyone in the nation *equal* opportunity irrespective of class, colour or creed, the Home Office document supplies an information pack on British government, social and welfare infrastructure and workplace rules. It outlines the basic knowledge that one requires to survive in the UK, and it is on this that aspiring citizens are examined in the citizenship test. The test is a Highway Code to good civic identity and practice. It does not convey the racial tensions in British life, the persisting real levels of inequality between the classes, the continuing resentment of English domination among many in the Celtic fringe, the more prominent feeling in England that the English must have their own Parliament and widespread uncertainty about the British role in Europe. Instead, the accent is upon keeping up appearances. Although fiction is acknowledged it is done so in parenthesis. The 'national story' invites the reader to infer that 'all will be for the best'. This has been a default position in British public culture since the Reform Acts of the nineteenth century. Nothing in these reflexive, interrogative, self-questioning times is more revealing about the general condition of British nationalism today.

## Nationalism-Strong/Nationalism-Lite

Traditionally, real, enduring identification with the nation involves a romantic attachment to blood and soil. It is a matter of regarding your life as one episode in the national story. The nation's 'skin' is your skin, the nation's interests are your interests, and an insult to the nation is a personal insult. As John of Gaunt said of England, in William Shakespeare's *Richard II* (Act 2, Scene 1):

> This royal throne of kings, this sceptred isle,
> This earth of majesty, this seat of Mars,
> This other Eden, demi-Paradise;

This fortress built by Nature for herself
Against infection and the hand of war;
This happy breed of men, this little world;
This precious stone set in the silver sea,
Which serves it in the office of a wall,
Or as moat defensive to a house,
Against the envy of less happier lands;
This blessed plot, this earth, this realm, this
England . . .

All of the key British traits of individualism, exceptionalism and 'chosen' status, to say nothing of the romantic national myth of genealogy, are present in this Elizabethan rhapsody on English nationalism. However, we know that strong attachment to nationalism is strongest when three conditions are met: 1) the population possesses stable lineage; 2) people are not mobile; and 3) where collective life is confronted with a tangible external threat.

These conditions are less prominent features of modern British life. One in ten Britons have a parent or grandparent born outside the nation. Metropolitan Britain is multi-ethnic, with different ethnic groups making demands to inflect traditional notions of Britishness through contrasting, distinctive cultural and political positions. The modern nation is increasingly mobile, and mass communication has made its people less insular. 63 per cent are regular Internet users (Ofcom 2007). The British travel abroad for their holidays in ever increasing numbers. The most recent figures on international air travel alone, supplied by National Statistics Online (www.statistics.gov.uk), prove unequivocally that Britain is a 'fortress' no more. Since 1984, the number of visits abroad made by UK residents has almost tripled to a record 64.2 million visits in 2004. Two-thirds of these were holidays, just under half of which were package holidays. 80 per cent of these visits abroad were to destinations in Europe, which again complicates the familiar canard from Brussels that the British are 'bad Europeans', who show no interest in the rest of the continent. Between July 2005 and July 2006, 67.7 million visits overseas were made by UK residents.

If this results in more and more of the population recognizing that Britain is not only the 'community among communities', but has always been a 'representation among representations', so much the better. British people still have pride in the nation and respect for its history and values. But the orthodox 'my country right or wrong' model that underpinned the traditional model of nationalism has declined. Globalization, multi-ethnicity and multiculturalism have thrust Britons into a condition in which most of them adopt a *strategic* attitude to national history and culture.

I call this condition 'nationalism-lite'. By this term, I mean a flexible, pragmatic relationship between individuals, groups and the nation. This contrasts sharply with the 'all or nothing' mentality of traditional, romantic British nationalism *a la* John of Gaunt in the passage from Shakespeare cited above. This traditional attitude might be called 'nationalism strong'. It requires individuals and groups to be ready to sacrifice tooth and claw for the nation. In contrast, 'nationalism-lite' is nationalism with conditions. For example, in the 1980s, during the long Thatcherite era, I was struck by how many of my academic friends, disenchanted with life in the old country, migrated to the Commonwealth and North America, and rapidly took dual citizenship – Australian, Canadian, New Zealander or American. This is what I mean by the 'pragmatic', 'flexible' or 'strategic' condition of 'nationalism-lite'. Their logic was faultless. Dual citizenship conferred tax breaks, welfare access and helped migrant children settle more quickly in schools. Even so, it struck me as coldly unsentimental and dispassionate about 'belonging' to the nation of one's birth. Lifestyle choices appeared to take precedence over nationalist loyalty. So much was this the case that identification with the nation seemed more like a marriage of convenience than a blood bond. My friends were not *positioned* by national belonging. They were *positioning* themselves to acquire market advantage and access to citizenship rights in nations to which they had migrated, that would otherwise have been denied to them.

Although it is inspired by deep religious conviction, I believe that the qualified attitude of many British Muslim fundamentalists to the British nation is of the same kidney. It is a flexible, strategic positioning with the motivation of gaining economic advantages and access to state citizenship and welfare rights. It is not an all or nothing commitment to the nation, as the widespread unhappiness and rejection of current British foreign policy in Afghanistan and Iraq plainly shows. 'Nationalism-lite' is at least as old as E. M. Forster's day. However, since then it has multiplied and spread, so that choosing your friend, or a tax break or welfare rights over your country, is no longer widely seen as shocking proof that you are not really 'one of us'.

On balance, I consider this a good thing. The emergence of 'nationalism-lite' reflects a more diverse, dynamic society, in which rights of citizenship are valued over Neanderthal nationalist loyalties. I believe it is healthier to respect – really respect – liberty, justice and democracy than to show blind obedience to the Union Jack. It is true that identifying with citizenship rights is less colourful than identifying with national culture and history. Convergence around citizenship rights as the foundation of belonging dilutes claims of national distinction. Yet it would be wrong to suggest that 'nationalism-lite' prohibits the expression of nationalist sentiment. When the British visit Spain, France, Germany, Italy and other countries in the European Union, they are aware of cultural difference and national distinction. 'Nationalism-lite' makes it a question of taste to display nationalist sentiment in determinate locations, such as a national sporting event, or the last night of the Proms, rather than uphold it as an unvarying, unerring feature of everyday life.

'Nationalism-lite' is the consequence of globalization, multi-ethnicity and multiculturalism. There is no turning back from this. The odds are very much in favour of the strengthening of these trends as overseas travel, migration, the expansion of mass communication and the greater enlargement and integration of the European Union continue apace. The 'precious stone set in a silver sea' cannot afford to be hard-hearted against migrants, the expansion of mass communication and the globalization of economy, culture and politics. In order to remain a force in the world, Britain has no choice but to be more inclusive and open. The 'moat' of former times has been breached, as much by national conscience in respect of its culture and history, mass communication and cheap air travel, as by immigration.

The 2004 Mori opinion poll drawing on focus groups in Chicago, Mumbai and Milan to provide attitudes on how others see the British and Britishness produced a stark identikit picture of the nation. To recap: the British are portrayed as clever, witty and possessed of a strong 'bulldog spirit'. They are regarded as a tolerant people with a deep respect for tradition. In contrast with other comparable nations, they are viewed as emotionally reserved, unduly proud of their heritage, more formal and slower to make friends. In addition, they are known for their poor dress sense and bad teeth.

If the British have learned to laugh at such stereotypes, it is a sign of cultural improvement. Inevitably, for a country that enjoyed such a long period of global domination, and whose language is the world's *lingua franca*, a great many myths have become encrusted around British values and ideals, its way of life and the course of its national history. Britain is not so much a community among communities – it is a representation among representations. The central characteristics of individualism, the rule of law, tolerance for dissent and respect for fair play are compatible with 'many Britains'. The challenge that we face is constructing new symbols that acknowledge the violence of class and racial privilege that have shaped British history for such a long time, while at the same time respecting the globalized, multicultural and multi-ethnic character of life in Britain today.

# Select Bibliography

Ackroyd, P., *Albion: The Origins of the English Imagination* (London, 2002)

Ajegbo, K., *Diversity and Citizenship Curriculum Review* (London, 2007)

Anderson, B., *Imagined Communities* (London, 1983)

Ashe, G., *Camelot and the Vision of Albion* (London, 1976)

Bakhtin, M., *Rabelais and his World* (Cambridge, 1968)

Bicheno, H., *Rebels and Redcoats* (London 2004)

Butler Report, *Review of Intelligence on Weapons of Mass Destruction*, www.butlerreview.org.uk (London, 2004)

Cannadine, D., 'Fantasy: Ian Fleming and the Realities of Escapism', in D. Cannadine, *In Churchill's Shadow* (Oxford, 2002), pp. 279–311

Cohen, R., 'Fuzzy Frontiers of Identity: The British Case,' Social Identities, 1 (1995), pp. 35–62

Colley, L., *Britons: Forging the Nation, 1707–1837* (New Haven, 1992)

Corrigan, P., and D. Sayer, *The Great Arch: English State Formation as Cultural Revolution* (Oxford, 1985)

Elkins, C., *Imperial Reckoning: The Untold Story of Britain's Gulag in Kenya* (London, 2005)

Ferguson, N., *Empire: How Britain Made the Modern World* (London, 2003)

Fox, K., *The English* (London, 2004)

Freud, S., *Civilization and its Discontents* (London, 1939)

Gane, M., ed., *Baudrillard Live* (London and New York, 1993)

Gellner, E., *Language and Solitude* (Cambridge, 1988)

—, *Nationalism* (London, 1997)

Giddens, A., *The Third Way* (Cambridge, 1998)

—, *The Third Way and its Critics* (Cambridge, 2000)

Gill, A. A., *The Angry Island* (London, 2005)

Gilroy, P., *After Empire: Melancholia or Convivial Culture* (London, 2004)

Hall, S., *The Hard Road To Renewal: Thatcherism and the Crisis of the Left* (London, 1988)

—, 'New Ethnicities', in *Race, Culture and Difference*, ed. J. Donald and A. Rattansi (London, 1992)

—, 'The West and the Rest: Discourses and Power', in *Formations of Power*, ed. S. Hall and B. Giben (Cambridge, 1992)

Haller, W., *Foxe's Book of Martyrs and the Elect Nation* (London, 1963)

Heath, A., R. Jowell and J. Curtice, *The Rise of New Labour* (Oxford, 2001)

Heath, A., C. Rothon and R. Andersen, *Who Feels British?*, Sociology Working Papers (2005), Dept of Sociology. Oxford University, www.sociology.ox.ac.uk

Hill, C., *A Turbulent, Seditious and Factious People: John Bunyan and his Church* (Oxford, 1988)

—, *The World Turned Upside Down* (Harmondsworth, 1972)

Holmes, R., *Sahib: The British Soldier in India* (London, 2005)

Hutton Inquiry, *Inquiry into the Circumstances Surrounding the Death of Dr David Kelly*, www.the-hutton-inquiry.org.uk (London, 2004)

Mann, M., *Incoherent Empire* (London, 2005)

Mitford, N., ed., *Noblesse Oblige* (London, 1956)

Orwell, G., *The Collected Essays, Journalism and Letters*, vol 2: *My Country Right or Left* (Harmondsworth, 1968)

Paine, T., *Common Sense* [1776] (New York, 1997)

—, *The Rights of Man* [1791–2] ( London, 1984)

Parekh, B., et al., *The Future of Multi-Ethnic Britain* (London, 2000)

Park, A., *British Social Attitudes: The 23rd Report, National Centre for Social Research* (London, 2007)

Pearson, G., *Hooligan: A History of Respectable Fears* (Basingstoke, 1983)

Potter, D., *The Glittering Coffin* (London, 1960)

Scheler, M., *Ressentiment* (New York, 1961)

Schmidt, H. D. 'The Idea and Slogan of "Perfidious Albion"', *Journal of the History of Ideas*, XIV/4 (1953), pp. 604-16

Thompson, E. P., *The Making of the English Working Class* (Harmondsworth, 1963)

Williams, R., *Keywords* (London, 1988)

Winder, S., *The Man Who Saved Britain* (London, 2006)

Wright, P., *On Living in an Old Country* (London, 1985)

# Photo Acknowledgements

The author and publishers wish to express their thanks to the below sources of illustrative material and/or permission to reproduce it:

photos Library of Congress, Washington, DC: pp. 8 (British Cartoon Prints Collection), 47 (Office of War Information, Overseas Picture Division, Washington Division), 71 photo of mural in Boston Public Library (Prints and Photographs Division), 89 (Office of War Information, Overseas Picture Division, Washington Division, courtesy of the United Nations Information Office, New York), 170 (Prints and Photographs Division), 208 (Prints and Photographs Division); photos Rex Features: pp. 23 (Rex Features/Richard Young), 66 (Rex Features/Sonny Meddle), 184 (Rex Features/Tim Rooke).

215